The Woman
God Created
You to Be

NOVELS BY
KIMBERLA LAWSON ROBY

THE REVEREND CURTIS BLACK SERIES

Casting the First Stone

Too Much of a Good Thing

The Best-Kept Secret

Love and Lies

Sin No More

The Best of Everything

Be Careful What You Pray For

Love, Honor, and Betray

The Reverend's Wife

A House Divided

The Prodigal Son

The Ultimate Betrayal

A Sinful Calling

Sin of a Woman

Better Late Than Never

STANDALONE TITLES

Behind Closed Doors

Here and Now

It's a Thin Line

A Taste of Reality

Changing Faces

One in a Million

A Deep Dark Secret

Secret Obsession

The Perfect Marriage

A Christmas Prayer

Best Friends Forever

Copycat

The Woman God Created You to Be

Finding Success Through Faith—
Spiritually, Personally,
and Professionally

KIMBERLA LAWSON ROBY

LENOX PRESS

Published by Lenox Press, P.O. Box 1264, Belvidere, IL 61008-1237

This book is intended to provide helpful and informative material on the subjects addressed in the publication. It is being made available with the understanding that the author and publisher are not engaged in rendering medical, health, mental health or any other kind of personal professional services in the book. The reader should consult his or her medical, health, mental health or other competent professional before adopting any of the suggestions in this book or drawing inferences from it.

Scripture quotations marked KJV are taken from the King James Version (KJV): King James Version, public domain.

Scripture quotations marked (NLT) are taken from the Holy Bible, New Living Translation, copyright ©1996, 2004, 2015 by Tyndale House Foundation. Used by permission of Tyndale House Publishers, Inc., Carol Stream, Illinois 60188. All rights reserved.

Scripture quotations marked (NIV) are taken from the Holy Bible, New International Version®, NIV®. Copyright © 1973, 1978, 1984, 2011 by Biblica, Inc.™ Used by permission of Zondervan. All rights reserved worldwide. www.zondervan.com. The "NIV" and "New International Version" are trademarks registered in the United States Patent and Trademark Office by Biblica, Inc.™

Scripture quotations taken from the New American Standard Bible® (NASB), copyright © 1960, 1962, 1963, 1968, 1971, 1972, 1973, 1975, 1977, 1995 by The Lockman Foundation. Used by permission. www.Lockman.org.

Scripture quotations marked ESV are from the ESV® Bible (The Holy Bible, English Standard Version®), copyright © 2001 by Crossway, a publishing ministry of Good News Publishers. Used by permission. All rights reserved.

Scripture quotations marked NKJV are from the New King James Version®. Copyright © 1982 by Thomas Nelson, Inc. Used by permission. All rights reserved.

Scripture quotations marked MSG are taken from *THE MESSAGE*, copyright © 1993, 2002, 2018 by Eugene H. Peterson. Used by permission of NavPress. All rights reserved. Represented by Tyndale House Publishers, Inc.

Front Cover Photo by © Sonya Martin

ISBN (paperback): 978-0-9653470-7-5
ISBN (ebook): 978-0-9653470-9-9

Library of Congress Cataloging-in-Publication Data

Name: Roby, Kimberla Lawson, author.
Title: The woman God created you to be: finding success through faith—spiritually, personally and professionally / Kimberla Lawson Roby
Identifiers:
Library of Congress Control Number: 2019916647
ISBN: 978-0-9653470-7-5

Printed in the United States of America

To my hearts and joy—

The amazing women who raised me:

My dear, sweet mom,
Arletha Tennin Stapleton

and

My dear, sweet
maternal grandmother,
Mary Tennin

Thank you for loving me so
unconditionally... for teaching me
such strong Christian values... and
for inspiring me with your incredible
strength, courage, and wisdom—all
of which helped me become the
woman I am today.

My Prayer for You
and Your Reading Journey

Father God, I come to You as humbly as I know how, thanking You for the woman who is preparing to read this book. I pray You will allow her to do so with an open and receptive heart, and that every word she reads will become a wonderful blessing to her. I pray these words will assist her in every way possible—spiritually, personally, and professionally—and that while reading them, she will feel Your wonderful presence the entire time. And most of all, dear Lord, I pray this book—every single chapter—will help her become all that *You* want her to be. Father, I thank You, and I ask You for these and all other blessings, in Your Son Jesus's name. Amen.

Kimberla

CONTENTS

PART THREE

THE PROFESSIONAL YOU

The Woman
God Created
You to Be

A Question Every Woman Should Ask Herself

Are you the *real* woman God created you to be? Have you wanted to become her? Have you wondered how to make that happen? If so, then you're the amazing woman I wrote this book for. You're the woman who wants to become even better than she already is. What you want is to become the *best* you can be in all areas of your life.

But, first, I think it's only fair that I answer the opening question myself.

So here goes ... For longer than I realized, I *wasn't* being the real woman God created me to be. Not spiritually, personally, or professionally. I mean, don't get me wrong, I have always loved, honored, and trusted God, and even though I have sometimes failed at it, I have also tried to be a great wife, daughter, sister, bonus mom, nana, aunt, niece, and friend. I've tried to be a great business professional, too. Still, I wasn't being the true woman that God wanted me to be.

But how could I?

Especially when it was years before I discovered that attending church on Sundays wasn't enough—and that building and maintaining my own personal relationship with God, and reading His Word, were the keys to becoming … the real woman He wanted me to be.

Had I been completely focused on my relationship with God from the time I entered adulthood, would I have become angry with Him when my mom became terminally ill? Would I have lost faith in Him to some degree? Would I have told myself that I would never be able to go on without her? Would I have struggled to forgive people who hurt me and held grudges against them for years? Would I have judged others when I had my own flaws and faults to work on? Would I have had sex before marriage? Would I have allowed all the rejection letters I received for my first book to discourage me from trying to get published? Would I have allowed fear to cripple me more times than I care to remember—as a woman, a writer, and a speaker? Would I have used even one word of profanity in the first few books I wrote? Or at times, would I have spoken those very words from my own mouth when I was infuriated with or hurt by someone? Would I have plastered a huge smile across my face while attending certain events, when deep down, I couldn't have been more exhausted and unhappy with parts of my career? Would I have allowed anxiety to hinder my emotional well-being?

So, yes, there was a time when I certainly was *not* being the real woman God wanted me to be.

As a matter of fact, in 2013, after writing twenty novels and being a *New York Times*, *USA Today*, *Essence*, *Washington Post*, *Dallas Morning News*, and *Publishers Weekly* best-selling author, I woke up one morning barely able to breathe. Not because I had medical issues, but because I no longer loved what I was doing. To be honest, I had nearly begun to despise it. I'd even begun shedding tears on far too many occasions, both publicly and privately, even though, for the most part, I smiled brightly for my reading audience and the media, just as everyone expected me to. I pretended that having a successful novel-writing career still made me happy, when Lord knows it didn't.

But, nonetheless, I did what most people do when they rise before dawn every single morning, year after year, preparing to go to a job they literally can't stand: I kept *doing* what I couldn't stand and wrote seven more fictional stories in total misery. I realize now, though, that I did what I thought I *had* to do, partly because so many of my loyal readers regularly asked when my next Reverend Curtis Black title or one of my standalone novellas would be hitting bookstores, and partly because, well ... writing fiction was how I earned my living. But let me tell you something right now. Something you've likely heard many times before.

Not *all* money is good money.

I'm a living witness to it.

I do want to be clear about something else, too, though. I did still love, love, love writing, but it was just that I no longer enjoyed creating fictional characters and storylines—at least not in the way I once had. In all truthfulness, I was totally burned out. I wasn't sure why, either, but as I forced myself to write and submit those last seven books to my publisher, my dear husband, Will, became concerned. He noticed how stressed and tired I was all the time. And while Will is my greatest supporter and always has been, he even suggested that, for a while, maybe I should write only one book per year instead of two, or that I should take a break altogether.

Now, one would think that if the man I love with my entire being gave me some much-needed advice, I would take it—and anyone who knows me personally knows that I definitely love

Will Roby with everything in me. But, like many super-*shero* kind of women I know, I thought I was fine and that I could easily handle the insane schedule I kept myself on. So much so that not even the alarming panic attack that sent me to the emergency room was enough to stop me. (Will and I didn't leave the ER until around midnight that night, yet I still boarded a plane the very next morning for a speaking engagement—with shortness of breath and heart palpitations. But I'll share more about this kind of foolish decision-making later.)

After that, though, I did take my doctor's advice and slowed down a bit. But sadly, it wasn't long before self-care became a distant memory, and I eased myself back to the norm. Soon I became more miserable than I had ever been in my life.

But then, something great happened.

God began speaking to my heart daily. Well, actually, what I know now is that He'd always been speaking to me, even through my thoughts, and that the only difference was that I was finally listening. I was also learning a lot more about discernment and how to hear His voice—something we should always pray for.

But He spoke to me and reminded me of the additional calling He had for my life, the one He'd revealed to me as early as October 2004. I know the month and year because this was when I had immediately searched online and purchased three books on professional speaking. Yes, I knew He still wanted me to write, but He also wanted me to use my gift and love for words to speak to women. He wanted me to use my own struggles, mistakes, and accomplishments to encourage women to seek Him first and to inspire them to become the great women He created them to be—spiritually, personally, and professionally.

But here's the thing. While I so wish I could tell you that this God-fearing girl hurried to answer His call, I didn't. Worse, I even went as far as telling Him what *I* thought about every bit of it, which was: "I'll do whatever You want me to do, but what else You got? Because speaking formally on a regular basis isn't something I see myself doing. It's not even something I *want* to be doing."

Still, He wouldn't take the calling away, and as weeks, months, and years passed, I went to bed with it, and I woke up with it... every... single... day.

Okay, so I think I need to repeat that part again, because my guess is that you, my dear sister in Christ, are doing the exact same thing. You're hesitant and likely even terrified of the idea of moving forward to fulfill the amazing purpose that God has so divinely and specifically assigned to you. So, I repeat: He wouldn't take it away, and as weeks, months, and years passed, I went to bed with it, and I woke up with it... every... single... day. Then, three years ago, I began going to bed and waking up... every... single... day with yet another assignment. This time it involved writing the book you're reading now—my first nonfiction title. I didn't see this happening, either, but again, it wouldn't go away. So, of course, this became the season in my life when I fully realized, more than ever before, that God always gets what He wants. We can try to ignore His call, we can run from it, and we can even pray with all our might for Him to eliminate it. But the truth of the matter is, God has created each of us in a unique fashion. He has given every one of us gifts, talents, and abilities, and just as God told Jeremiah, He knew who we were going to be well before the day we were born.

"Before I shaped you in the womb, I knew all about you.
Before you saw the light of day, I had holy plans for you:
A prophet to the nations—that's what I had in mind for
you."
                    —JEREMIAH 1:5 (MSG)

God knew, and while you and I may not have known for
years what plans He had for us—or maybe you still don't fully
know now—what I can promise you is this: Your purpose has
always been there. It has been present in your heart, soul, and
spirit. I know this, because while I didn't write my first book
until I was thirty years old, there was no denying that from the
time I was in elementary school, I had a great love for writing.
Then, even though I didn't see myself speaking in front of hundreds of people, Mrs. Ceola Pearson, the children's director at
the church I was born into, did. Why? Because, as a child, if
I was given a short Easter speech to recite instead of a longer
one, I was *not* happy. Mrs. Pearson never forgot that, and just a
year or so before she passed (forty-plus years after I delivered
those childhood speeches), she shared that story with Will.
He'd been visiting her and one of his friends (her son), and
when he returned home, he told me how they'd laughed about
it and how she'd also brought up the fact that I had *always*
had a lot to say. I laughed, too, and while I hadn't thought
about it before, it was then that I realized how perfectly God
had placed the wonderful Mrs. Pearson at the forefront of my
purpose, many years before I knew what that purpose was
going to be. When I was just a small girl, not only had Mrs.
Pearson given me my very first opportunities to speak, she'd
also given me the courage to do so, and she'd taught me how

to deliver those speeches in front of our entire congregation, which meant that from the very beginning, I'd learned how to speak from a faith-based perspective.

Then, there was my dear mom and dear maternal grandmother, who taught me to love and honor God, no matter what. I was a small girl then, too, but as soon as I was old enough to understand, they taught me about believing in God and about accepting Jesus Christ as my personal Savior. They raised me to have strong Christian, moral, and family values, and it is because of the two of them that I have spent so much of my life trying to do the right thing, as well as trying to treat others the way I want to be treated.

Please do understand, though, that I certainly haven't always been successful in my attempts. Please know, too, that I've done and said things I wish I could take back—things I'm absolutely not proud of. But it is because of my Christian upbringing that I have still tried to honor God's Word. Not to mention, in those times when I haven't done the right thing or when I have said something terrible, I always knew right away that I was wrong, and I soon felt God's conviction. Sometimes I felt it immediately, or worse, I would feel convicted *before* I said or did the wrong thing, yet I would still say or do it anyway.

Now, how awful is that?

But, then, of course, like the good Christian girls that most of us try to be, I would ask God to forgive me. I would feel bad about it, too. Yet that didn't always stop me from repeating some of my same transgressions.

As I eased into my thirties, forties, and fifties, though—experiencing many types of disappointment and pain—I worked even harder to do the right thing. I also worked on my overall

relationship with God so that I wouldn't have to ask Him to forgive me for things I knew I shouldn't be doing or saying in the
first place. But are there still times when I fall short of His
glory? Absolutely. Am I perfect in any way, shape, or form?
Definitely not.

And I never will be.

But the point I'm trying to make here is that I have willingly
made a conscious effort to grow in Him and become the true
woman He created me to be. This is crucial for all women, and I
am forever grateful to my mom and grandmother—two precious
women of God—for starting me on a faith-driven path as early
as possible.

This is also the reason that I have written this book in
three sections: *The Spiritual You*, *The Personal You*, and *The
Professional You*. Because what I've learned more than anything else, as it relates to becoming the great women that God
wants us to be, is that we need to have not one or two but all
three areas of our lives in order. First and foremost, we need
to make sure that we have solid spiritual well-being, because
without God, nothing else will work properly anyhow. Then,
once we have our spiritual lives in order, we need to make sure
that we're taking care of ourselves from a personal standpoint,
physically and mentally, and we also need to make sure that
our relationships with our husbands or the men we're dating as
well as our relationships with our family members and friends
are healthy. From there, we can work on being who we need to
be in our professional arenas. Because whether God has called
us to work in ministry, start our own businesses, work in the
public sector or in corporate America, being professional is

very necessary, and we need to keep our faith at the center of all of it.

So, with that said, once you've finished reading this book, my hope is that you will know, beyond a shadow of a doubt, what steps to take to become the *real* woman God created you to be. My prayer is that your spiritual, personal, and professional lives will become so aligned and so in balance that you will be happier than you've ever been. My prayer is that you'll arrive at a point in your life where you won't have to smile to keep from crying, the way I used to. You'll smile because you're genuinely happy and bursting with incredible joy. But most of all, my prayer is that you will become totally equipped and ready to serve others in a way like never before—because serving and helping others is what matters more than anything I can think of.

And this, my dear sister, is what God wants from all of us.

PART ONE

THE SPIRITUAL YOU

CHAPTER 1

Having a True Relationship with God— and Not Just on Sunday

When my mom was six months pregnant with me, her husband went missing. It wasn't because someone kidnapped him, either. He just up and left one day—with no warning, no goodbye, no anything. Worse, he even took the little bit of money they'd stashed away for the baby they were expecting. My own biological father did this. He abandoned my then twenty-year-old mother while she was working, and she never saw him again.

Until twenty-two years later.

This was also the first time that he and I had ever laid eyes on each other, which only happened because of a gentleman I'd met at my mom's eldest sister's house. One Saturday afternoon, I'd gone to visit my dear aunt Mary Lou and dear uncle Charlie, and as it had turned out, a friend of my father's was visiting from Chicago, and when the gentleman learned who my father was, he said, "Your dad lives right around the corner from me."

Needless to say, I was stunned, curious, and excited about the possibility of finally meeting the father I had always wondered about. The man I had always wanted to see but had never as much as spoken to by phone. Still, I couldn't help pondering the fact that, all this time, he'd been living only ninety miles away from me. My father had resided so close to

Rockford, Illinois, that it would have taken him no more than maybe an hour and a half to drive there, yet he hadn't tried to see me even once?

But nonetheless, as hard as this was for me to accept, I still couldn't wait to connect with him. So, I gave the gentleman my phone number and asked him to pass it on to my father. He did exactly that, and my father called me two days later. It was a good conversation, too. I'm not sure how I expected to feel, but for whatever reason, my heart wouldn't allow me to be angry at him. Then, after we'd been communicating for a few months, I learned that I would be going to Chicago to take a state employment exam, so I asked him if he wanted to meet at the State Building. He was beyond happy about the idea, and my dear, sweet mom even offered to take a vacation day from work so she could accompany me for support.

Both my parents have been deceased for a while now—my father passed in 1989, two years after I met him, and my mom passed away in 2001, when I was only thirty-six years old. But from time to time, I still think about how kind it was for my mom to go with me to meet my father. I also think about the fact that she never badmouthed him to me one single time. She'd certainly told me how devastated and heartbroken she'd been when he'd deserted her—and how she'd had no idea what she and I were going to do—but again, she never spoke against him as my father. Then, as if that hadn't been enough, on the day she and I drove over to Chicago, she sat in the food court with him while I took my exam. She hadn't seen or heard from him in more than two decades, yet she laughed and talked with him as if they were good friends. She sat in the company of a man who'd left her with no other choice but to move back home with her parents—parents who had quickly come to her rescue, telling her that everything would be all right and then welcoming her and her unborn baby with such wonderful love and compassion. In fact, right after my mom had given birth to me, those same parents had paid the hospital fifty dollars, something that had been required before my mom and I could leave the maternity ward. My grandparents would always tell me that story with huge smiles on their faces: "We had to pay fifty dollars just to bring you home," and to this day, I am forever grateful to them for becoming my second parents—until the moment they each took their last breaths—and for making such an amazing difference in my life.

But again, that day I took my employment exam, my mom sat chatting with her ex-husband as though they had never lost touch with each other. My mom had forgiven a man who'd never offered her a single dime of child support. A man who hadn't as much as contacted her to ask if his daughter needed anything—in twenty-two years. Although, as I got older, I did learn from my grandmother that when I was a toddler, my father had called *her*, basically saying that he was down on his luck, moneywise, and that this was the reason he didn't want to see me. My grandmother, of course, had reminded him that I was being well taken care of.

To this day, I'm not sure exactly how much my grandmother told my father, but what I do know is that before I turned three years old, my mom married my stepdad, a hardworking man who became the only dad I had ever known, and to me, he *was* my dad. I also had the best aunties and uncles any child could want, my mom's ten siblings. So, just as my grandmother had told my father, I truly was being well taken care of. My parents weren't rich by any stretch of the imagination, but if you were to ask most people about the Midwest and how it was back in the sixties and seventies, they would tell you that it was very common for both parents to be working on assembly lines at factories, and that they earned a good living.

My dad worked for Chrysler Corporation, and my mom worked for a company called Atwood Industries, and all I knew was that I never went without anything. I also never had to wait until payday to get the things I needed, and there was a strong household emphasis placed on saving money, both at a bank and at a credit union. My parents also purchased their first home when I was five, and my maternal grandparents moved in with us. Sometimes now, though, I do laugh because as a child, I didn't know we weren't "well off." Which just goes to show that you don't have to be filthy rich to be happy, comfortable, and content.

But nonetheless, my grandmother went on to tell my father that regardless of whether he had anything to give me or not, I needed to know who my father was. She tried her best to make him understand that my seeing him was more important than anything else. But soon, he stopped calling, and that was the end of it—until twenty-plus years later.

And have I mentioned how my mom told me that when I was born, she'd taken one look at me and decided that I hadn't asked for any of this? And that if she could help it, I would never spend one day on welfare? Did I mention how she went to work in a factory on May 20, 1965—just seventeen days after I was born? And that she remained employed at that same company until she passed away thirty-six years later, rarely missing a day and never being late? Or how about the fact that when she started working there, she earned only $1.60 an hour, yet she still paid my grandmother every Friday, without fail, for babysitting me? And she also saved five dollars each Friday in her credit union savings account? Or the fact that her twin brother, my dear, kind uncle Ben, bought her first car for her so she would have transportation to work? Or how, even though my dear, devoted aunt Mary Lou worked nights, she would pick up my grandmother and me—because as a baby I was very sickly—to take me to lots of doctor's appointments, so that my mom wouldn't have to miss work or lose her job?

But again, she hadn't seen my father in twenty-two years.

Not in all that time, yet my beautiful mom still smiled when she saw him. She never asked him why he'd walked out on us, she didn't judge him, and most of all, she didn't resent him. Not the way I eventually did. Remember earlier when I said I hadn't felt any anger toward my father? The first time I had spoken to him? Well, over the next few months, I couldn't stop thinking about the way he'd left my mom and how he hadn't done anything for me or tried to see me, and I didn't call him as much— even though he still called me—and the second and only other time I saw him alive was when he came to Rockford for my grandmother's homegoing service. Then, the third and final time I saw him was at his own service in Chicago. This was also when I finally got a chance to meet some of my other relatives on his side of the family. But as time passed, I regretted not forgiving him the way my mom had, and if I could do things over, I would call him and spend as much time with him as possible, the entire two years. Had my relationship with God been where it is today, I would have had a lot more compassion for him and understood that everyone makes mistakes. I would have forgiven him a lot sooner than I had, well before he passed away, instead of a few years afterward, and cherished the short time we had left together.

But again, my mom didn't judge or resent my father, and this was one of those times in my mom's life (and there were many) when I realized just how huge her heart was. It was then, too, that I began paying a lot more attention to how forgiving she was, and I also paid attention to the kind of relationship she had with God. I noticed how she truly did try to treat others the way she wanted to be treated, even when people hurt or betrayed her.

My grandparents had raised their children to love and honor God, and while I realize no one is perfect, my mom was a great woman. Like her own mother, she was loving, caring, and full of wisdom, and the two of them were everything I could have hoped for.

To me, they were the best mother and grandmother ever.

And my grandfather was the best grandfather—the absolute *best* man I knew until the day he passed away.

And I loved the three of them with all my heart and soul.

Still, there was more. Something else that made an even greater difference in our lives.

My grandmother was a God-fearing woman who carried my mom and her siblings to church from the time they began growing in her womb.

My mom carried my two brothers and me to church in her womb, too. Not all at the same time, of course. But my point is that my dear brothers (Willie and Michael) and I have been attending church since before our mom gave birth to us. Our foundation was established very early on, and I am so truly grateful to her for that.

Then, as I grew older, she and my grandparents taught me more and more about God, and by the time I was seven, I couldn't wait to officially join our church and become baptized (this is standard protocol in the Baptist faith). I could also finally take communion, and I couldn't wait to become active in our children's department—I couldn't wait to join the Angelic Choir with my dear first cousin Patricia, something that became the highlight of my early childhood years. After that, Patricia and I became junior ushers, and then at age thirteen, I became a member of the Imperial Choir, which was *the* choir that most of the youth in our church were excited to join. This is likely the reason, too, that to this day, I am still a huge lover of gospel music, and when I hear certain songs, I feel such extreme joy that tears fill my eyes and stream down either side of my face. This experience happens in church, of course, but sometimes it happens right in my own home or in my car while I'm driving. Sometimes it happens as I'm pulling up next to someone at a stoplight, which is when I immediately begin hoping that the other driver doesn't glance over at me, wondering if I'm in desperate need of help. Why? Because sometimes, my crying isn't subtle. Sometimes certain gospel songs will touch my soul so beautifully and so intensely that I do the ugly cry. I literally become that emotional.

And beyond happy.

Gospel music also has a noticeable way of keeping me focused on my faith and my relationship with God. Not just on Sunday, but on every day of the week. I also pray and talk to Him about everything. After all these years, I still recite the Lord's Prayer daily, the same as I was taught to do as a child. But as an adult, when I'm finished saying it, I also continue praying in my own words. I thank God for waking me up in my right mind (something my grandmother thanked God for every single morning) and in good health. I thank Him for allowing me to see yet another day. I thank Him for all He's done, all He's doing, and all He's going to do—I thank Him for His unconditional love, mercy, and grace. I pray for Will, myself, and each and every one of our biological family members, as well as the people we consider to be our family. I pray for all of our friends, our pastor, our pastor's wife, their children, and our entire church family. I pray for our neighbors and all my readers. I pray for people we know as acquaintances as well as people we have never met. I also pray for anyone who has asked me to pray for a specific problem, struggle, or illness. I ask God to heal all those who are sick—spiritually, mentally, emotionally, and physically. I ask Him to give strength, comfort, peace, and understanding to those who have lost loved ones—whether they've lost them recently, in the past few months, or many years ago. I ask God to please protect all of us, every human being alive, and to keep us safe and free of all harm and danger. I ask Him to provide peace and unity, here in the United States and throughout the world. I ask Him for all of this in His Son Jesus's name. I do this because of John 14:14 (KJV), which states: "If ye shall ask any thing in my name, I will do it." This is one of my favorite scriptures, and I have it taped on one of the upper cabinets of my desk credenza in my office.

I also make sure to tell our dear Heavenly Father how much I love, honor, and worship Him. I tell Him just how much I believe in Him, trust in Him, and depend on Him, and how I have total and complete faith in Him.

I do this daily.

But, unfortunately, this wasn't always the case. Yes, as a child, I was taught very well in this respect, yet as an adult, I didn't always have the genuine kind of relationship with God that I should. The reason? For many years, I went to church mainly because I was taught to do so, and not necessarily to praise and worship God with everything in me.

To be honest, I rarely opened the Bible I kept at home, which meant that the only time I did open and read a Bible was on Sunday mornings during church service. Then, as far as my prayer life went, I knew to get down on my knees to pray at night before getting in bed, because again, I'd been taught to do so. But that was basically it. In fact, once I entered my twenties and I was no longer living in my childhood home, where my mom or grandmother could witness it, I slowly but surely resorted to saying my prayers while lying in bed, and sometimes I forgot to say them at all. Not because I didn't want to. It was just that I'd become far too lax with the idea of jumping straight into bed and dropping off to sleep.

I do want to state this, however: I honestly believe it is perfectly fine to pray in any position—standing, sitting, kneeling, or lying. It is true that I do sometimes prefer going into one of our small upstairs closets, shutting the door, reading scripture, and praying in total seclusion, but I also know that God hears every one of our prayers, regardless of when, where, and how we say them. What He wants is for us to communicate with Him regularly and sincerely.

From our hearts.

Our souls.

Often.

What He wants is for us to acknowledge Him at all times and to know that only *He* can bring us through whatever difficulties we are experiencing. He wants us to understand that we cannot do *anything* without Him.

Even when my mom arrived home from work all those years ago and learned that her husband was gone, one of the first things my grandmother told her was "God is going to take care of you and your baby. You're going to be fine." Every now and then, my grandmother would tell me that story, too—what it was like when she and my grandfather arrived at my mom's house that afternoon—and as I type these words, I can't help shedding tears. Partly because of how sad it makes me when I think just how broken my mom must have been, and partly because of how happy I am to know just how right my grandmother was.

God truly did take care of my mom and me.

God does what He says He will do, and while I never asked my mom, I'm sure her devastating experience drew her much closer to God than she ever had been. It likely pushed her relationship with Him to a much higher level. This also might be the reason that when I was in my twenties, my mom realized she needed to have an important conversation with me. A conversation I wasn't expecting. You see, I believed my mom could make everything better. Absolutely *everything*. To me, she always had, and it was the reason I always went to her when I was troubled. But one day, I called her about something upsetting, and she said, "I've noticed that whenever you have a problem or if something is really bothering you, you call *me* before going to God with it. So, you need to start going to Him first."

Really?

I mean, I definitely knew how important it was to pray, but I won't deny it, I was a little shocked, hurt, and confused by what my mom was saying, because not once had she ever *not* given me the advice I asked her for. I saw her nearly every day, and on the days I didn't, we would chat by phone, sometimes two to three times—every single day.

But God knows what we need, now and in the future. Because, little did I know, it wouldn't be more than ten years later that my mom would be gone, and I would find myself needing God more than ever.

I would need Him in ways I hadn't considered, and it is because of my mom that I began going to Him for everything the way she'd told me. My mom is the reason that my relationship with God became my top priority and how I made it through the most painful period of my life. Because Lord knows, I'd had no idea that my mom, the strongest woman I knew—my best friend in the world—would become ill and pass away at the young age of fifty-seven years old. No one could have told me that my entire world would completely shatter into pieces. I just wouldn't have imagined it, and I'm really going to have to prepare myself before sharing the rest of this story with you a little later.

But, for now, just know this: Having a solid relationship with God is very necessary. Not just on Sundays, but daily.

Three hundred sixty-five days per year.

And how do we accomplish this?

By reading His Word, praying to Him, talking to Him, trusting Him, and depending on Him.

By giving Him our time and attention—the kind He so wonderfully deserves.

THREE THINGS YOU CAN DO

1. Find a proper church home.

Six years ago, Will and I began attending a new church, which is led by a pastor who both teaches and delivers his sermons. Will and I love that about him, and we also love that we found a pastor who has great integrity, love for his wife and family, and love for people everywhere, regardless of who they are. In fact, we attended our church home for nearly two years before officially joining as new members. We did this because we wanted to be sure about moving our membership, especially since we had attended our former church for decades. Also, while Will and I have always been members of the Baptist faith, we don't focus on the idea of denomination. So, even if our church were nondenominational, our Christian values, belief, and faith would remain the same. The other thing to remember, too, is that, yes, we can pray and worship God *anywhere*, and we can also do it alone. But doing so with others through fellowship at a Bible-based church is a truly wonderful thing and something we look forward to.

2. Build and maintain a solid relationship with God.

This is key. I communicate with God multiple times per day, Monday through Sunday, through prayer, song, and conversation. Sometimes I talk to Him out loud, even. Sometimes I will stop in the middle of what I'm doing just so I can ask Him how I should handle a certain situation. Many times, I will ask Him to guide me in my decision-making. Sometimes I'll ask Him to give me peace about something. Or sometimes I'll just thank Him for giving me a wonderful husband, family, and friends. I talk to Him about everything, and I am a better person because of it. I also want to reiterate that I pray every single day, because this truly makes a great difference for me, and I know it will for you, too.

3. Read and study your Bible.

Doing this has changed my life. First, I began selecting a certain book of the Bible to read, and then I would read one full chapter per day and think about what that chapter means. But I'll be honest, there were days when I missed doing so. Then, eventually, I realized that reading even one verse, meditating on it and truly taking it to heart, helps me a great deal. And although I am still very much surprised by this, I suddenly lost my desire to read as many novels as I used to, and instead, I gained a great love for inspirational nonfiction. I also keep two separate daily devotionals on my nightstand. Sometimes I read them in the morning, and sometimes at night, but these two books guide me and keep me encouraged as well. Attending Bible study at church or online is another great way to learn and discuss God's Word, and it is something I need to make time for in my schedule. I have been saying this for a while now, because great Bible teachers can enlighten you in ways that you might not experience on your own. Something else that Will and I do, too, is watch church programs and Christian talk shows on Daystar and TBN.

A SCRIPTURE TO HELP YOU

"Love the Lord your God with all your heart and with all your
soul and with all your mind."

—MATTHEW 22:37 (NIV)

CHAPTER 2

Church People

In January 2000, my third book, *Casting the First Stone,* was released. It centered on a fictitious character named Reverend Curtis Black. Of course, as with each book I have written, I was excited to be embarking on my national book tour, and I was even more excited to meet and spend time with my amazing readers. But as Will and I traveled around the country attending events, I realized that most of my readers, in every city, had one particular thing in common. They all knew who Reverend Curtis Black was. They'd experienced him, or at the very least, they'd heard of this type of pastor—one who was consumed with money, power, and women. A man who proudly stood in his pulpit on Sunday mornings delivering infamous do-as-I-say-not-as-I-do weekly sermons. A man who committed sin after sin simply because he believed he could do whatever he wanted as long as he repented and prayed about it later. A man who continued to sin and hurt a great number of people, including his wife and children.

But more than that, what I discovered was that many of my readers knew Reverend Curtis Black so well that they began telling their own personal stories and sharing out loud the real names of their pastors. For a short while, I was stunned, but soon

I realized that, unfortunately, Reverend Curtis Black was alive and well in every single city in the country. What I ultimately came to terms with, too, was a very sad reality: Not every man or woman who declares that they have been called by God to preach truly has been, and not every person who portrays themselves as Christian actually is. Some are simply church people. Some are simply pretending to love and honor God because it makes them look good, and it allows them an opportunity to be seen in a certain way. They pretend to walk in an upright, decent, Christian, do-gooder sort of fashion. But behind closed doors, their conversation, moral values, and overall way of living are very different. Sometimes people who pray and worship in church on Sunday will curse you out on Monday and think nothing of it. Some won't even wait for that. Some will curse you out or "get you told" right in the church parking lot—on Sunday morning—if you cross them.

As far as writing an entire series about Reverend Curtis Black, church scandal, and corruption, though, I didn't do it to ridicule the church. I love God too much for that, and it was actually just the opposite. I wrote those fifteen books partly because after *Casting the First Stone*, my readers continued asking me for three years when I would be writing the sequel, but more than anything, I wrote them so that Christians everywhere would pay close attention to who their church leaders were. I wanted readers to be cautious and to not find themselves worshiping another human being simply because he or she was standing in a pulpit. My hope was that my readers would find a God-fearing pastor and make sure that their own personal relationships with God were intact (the way I talked about in Chapter 1). I certainly wanted them to read the Word for themselves.

I knew how important this was for all Christians, because as a woman who has attended church my entire life, I have seen and heard a lot. Yes, thankfully, there are thousands of wonderful pastors nationwide, but again, there are just as many Reverend Curtis Blacks in the world who are misleading lots of innocent people, and church hurt has become more common than ever before. Worse, I have heard some women say that because of their pastor's corrupt actions, they have decided to never attend church again. And this is the most heartbreaking part of all. It's tragic even, and sadly, some of the books I've written are meek and mild compared to some of the real-life stories I have been told.

I've heard many.

But there is one story I'll never forget—the one where a pastor's wife received a phone call from a dental office reminding her about her upcoming appointment. Normally, this kind of call wouldn't be out of the ordinary, except, this pastor's wife hadn't scheduled any dental appointments she was aware of. Long story short, what she soon discovered was that her well-known pastor husband was allowing his mistress to use his wife's name *and* their dental insurance for her own purposes. When I learned about this, I was near speechless, and while I do realize that pastors aren't perfect people, just as none of us are, I still believe that if you say you have been called by God to minister, there are some things you just shouldn't be doing. I believe you should hold yourself to a higher standard. I know not everyone agrees with that philosophy, but I believe that if God calls you to do something, you have a responsibility to uphold that calling in the most honorable way possible. To me, you should want to do nothing less.

"A church leader is a manager of God's household, so he must live a blameless life. He must not be arrogant or quick-tempered; he must not be a heavy drinker, violent, or dishonest with money. Rather, he must enjoy having guests in his home, and he must love what is good. He must live wisely and be just. He must live a devout and disciplined life."

—TITUS 1:7–8 (NLT)

But please let me say this. I am not stating any of the above to be judgmental or to sound self-righteous (you've already read how I've fallen short in many areas). Still, I do want to make sure I share certain realities. I'm doing this because my hope is that you will take some time to evaluate your own Christian walk. Why, you might ask? Because we all get used to what we get used to. We form lifelong habits without realizing it, and sometimes the only way we can determine what changes we need to make is to take a personal inventory. Assess our thoughts, words, and actions. Sometimes we need to ask ourselves in-depth questions.

We can do this for any problem at all, but for example, let's just say using profanity is something you struggle with. If so, you could begin by asking yourself the following: 1) Am I speaking the words "hallelujah," "praise God" or "thank you, Jesus," during church service, and then using every curse word known to mankind as soon as service is over? 2) Am I only using profanity every now and then, possibly only two to three times per year, and thinking that maybe there is nothing wrong with that? 3) Is there ever really a need for me to use curse words? 4) Do I use them because when I'm seething with anger,

I believe curse words will help me get my point across better?
5) Am I aware that, in most cases, what they do is turn minor
disagreements into full-blown confrontations? 6) Do I curse in
front of my children ... or in front of anyone else's children? 7) If
so, am I being a good example for them? 8) Am I living according to Ephesians 4:29 (NLT), which says: "Don't use foul or
abusive language. Let everything you say be good and helpful,
so that your words will be an encouragement to those who hear
them"? and 9) If I met Jesus face-to-face today, would I curse
in front of Him?

Because let's be honest. While Jesus certainly knows our
every thought, and He hears everything we say, would you curse
if He was *physically* sitting next to you? I know I wouldn't. But
unfortunately, there have been those rare occasions in my life
when someone would make me angry enough to spew a word or
two of profanity. I never did this in the presence of my parents,
grandparents, aunts, uncles, other elders, or children, because
I would never disrespect them that way. But, again, I have definitely said the occasional bad word. You know, like during the
early years of my marriage to Will, whenever we had heated
debates? Those that would sometimes become full-scale arguments? The kind where you both believe that you're right about
everything you're saying, and the other person is dead wrong—
and you both yell a few choice words at each other? Will and I
can laugh about those early years now, but today, I would tell any
married couple that none of this is necessary. I would tell them
that you can, in fact, disagree without using profanity or any
other offensive wording.

I'm embarrassed to say, too, that when I was in junior high
and high school, I would occasionally use curse words, right

along with other kids. And guess why? Because it was the "cool" and "very in" thing to do.

Still, I don't like cursing (not even on rare occasions the way I just spoke about). I didn't grow up hearing profanity in my household, and I don't prefer to hear it from others. It is the reason that I eventually arrived at a point in my life where, even if a profane word left my mouth only once or twice per year, I immediately felt bad about it. Even if no one other than Will or a friend could hear what I was saying, I felt embarrassed. It always seemed wrong. Which is why, to this very day, I am still ashamed of the fact that I used profanity in my first nine books—mainly because I told myself that I needed to stay true to the characters I was writing about—even though I wasn't okay with it. I convinced myself that if a character was evil or even if they were a good character who had been deeply hurt or betrayed, I needed to write the kind of true-to-life dialogue they would speak.

Even back then, though, my family members and friends would likely tell you that "Kim, doesn't curse." (They, of course didn't know about my cursing moments behind closed doors.) They would also tell you, "Whenever Kim hears anyone cursing in front of children, she will graciously remind them that children are present." Why? Because I believe we should present ourselves to our young people in a more suitable fashion. We should teach them to be the best that they can be. What I learned a long time ago, too, is that whenever I bring this to someone's attention, they don't seem offended, and they will usually apologize and say something such as "Oh, I'm sorry. I forgot kids were in the room." I have so much respect for people who respond in that manner, and some men (and some women, too) will even apologize for cursing in front of other adults when they know those adults don't use profanity, which I so very much appreciate, too.

Actually, I believe that most people do want to respect others, and of course, cursing certainly does not make anyone a bad person (some of the kindest and most caring people I know like to curse). But this book is about becoming the real woman God created you to be, and my goal is to help you accomplish that. Profanity may seem minor and no big deal because so many people use it, but it doesn't properly represent our Christian faith. It doesn't agree with Ephesians 4:29.

I'll tell you something else that I've done in my life, too, that I wish I hadn't. Something that, from a very young age, my mom and grandmother encouraged me not to do. They warned me about boys and told me that many of them only wanted one thing. But once I discovered that other girls were having sex, that made *me* curious about having sex, too. This is something I still shake my head at, because my mom had always told me to never be a follower. Always. And for the most part, I took her advice—but not when it came to having sex as a teenager. Then, when I became an adult, I didn't focus much on the fact that fornication was a sin. I definitely knew it was, but remember earlier when I talked about knowing better and still doing the wrong thing anyway? I mean, I definitely wasn't the kind of young woman who slept with lots and lots of men, but fornication is fornication. To me, sleeping with men outside of marriage, whether it's one man, five, or twenty, is equally wrong and requires the same level of repentance.

And here's another transparent part of my life that I want to share with you. Will and I *didn't* wait until we were married, either. We'd gone on our first date in May 1990 when I was twenty-five years old and he was thirty-six, but just one month later, he'd given up his apartment and moved into mine. But thank God, four months later in September we were married. Not everyone thought our marriage would last, because a four-month courtship isn't very long. But all we knew was that we were in love, and that we wanted to spend the rest of our lives together. That was twenty-nine years ago, and while it is true that the only reason we stopped fornicating was because we became husband and wife (and not because it was wrong), I am still grateful—grateful that this became one less sin we had to worry about. I was happy that we were no longer living in sin—fornicating and shacking up—all while attending church on Sundays and publicly portraying ourselves as "good" Christians.

And *you* don't have to falsely portray yourself, either.

Because whether you are fornicating, committing adultery, speaking harshly about others, dishonoring your mother or father, or stealing (and yes, this does include lifting paper clips and printing paper from your employer's office supply room and grabbing "extra" sugar packets from coffee shops for personal use at home—or not paying for anything else that you know you *should* have paid for)—if you are struggling with any kind of sin, even lying or using profanity—God will give you the strength to rise above all of it, and He will forgive you *completely.*

"He does not treat us as our sins deserve or repay us according to our iniquities. For as high as the heavens are above the earth so great is his love for those who

fear him; as far as the east is from the west, so far has he removed our transgressions from us."
—PSALM 103:10–12 (NIV)

It is true that we are all works in progress and we will never be blemish-free, but there is always room for improvement. We can always become better, and that's what I'm striving for.

We can become women who diligently seek Him.

We can become true Proverbs 31 women—the way He intended.

So much so that we won't have to say a word. Our family members, friends, and even strangers will know who we are simply by witnessing our actions. They'll know just from being in our presence. When someone lies on us, they will *know* that someone is lying on us, and they will readily defend us.

They will know that we are true Christian women.

And not just church people.

THREE THINGS YOU CAN DO

1. Listen to your conscience, and let it guide you.

Whenever I've done something that wasn't quite right, my conscience has bothered me. It has always let me know when I needed to stop doing something or if I needed to do something better. I am very much in tune with this, and I also believe that this is yet another way God speaks to us. We are free to do right or wrong, but if our hearts mean well and we genuinely want to become good Christians, God is always standing in the gap, waiting to help us. Doing the wrong thing can sometimes be very tempting, but as we grow in our faith and focus on our relationship with God, temptation becomes less and less. You arrive at a point where you don't want to do many of the things you once did. I used to hear my grandmother talk about that, and as sure as I am sitting here writing this, I am now a living witness to it. Certain likes and desires will vanish without warning, and you'll wonder why you ever wanted to do those things in the first place. You'll discover *new* likes and desires, those you can honestly feel good about.

2. Go to a quiet place.

I know I've talked a lot about my relationship with God (as well as your relationship with Him), but it's only because this is the one relationship that can help you with everything. So, as it relates to becoming a true Christian, taking *everything* to God is key. I've already mentioned how much I enjoy going into one of our small closets to read scripture and pray, and it is the reason I love Matthew 6:6 (NLT), which says, "But when you pray, go away by yourself, shut the door behind you, and pray to your Father in private. Then your Father, who sees everything, will reward you." But sometimes it's good to go there just to hear Him. Sometimes I will close my eyes, take a deep breath, ask Him a specific question, and wait for Him to answer. He will then either give me peace about something and confirmation to move forward or allow me to leave that closet feeling uncomfortable, which means that His answer is no, or not yet. But let's just say you want to stop badmouthing other women—just as an example. What you can do is go to your quiet place and ask God to remove that particular desire. Or maybe, as of today, you've decided to become celibate, and you want to remain that way until you're married. Maybe you no longer want to use the Lord's name in vain. Maybe you want to stop jeopardizing your health. Maybe you want to forgive someone the way God forgives us, but you've been struggling with it. Whatever it is, you can ask God about it and wait to hear from Him. You can be still and know that He is God, just as Psalm 46:10 tells us to. You can also begin by questioning yourself. Remember the in-depth questions I talked about earlier? Those we should sometimes ask ourselves—when we're having problems of any kind? But after doing that, please take your struggles and temptations to God, so that He can give you answers and the final direction you need.

3. Be the same person inside and outside of the church.

Many years ago, I attended a meeting with a small group of my elders—men and women who were old enough to be my parents and grandparents. These were people I had known most of my life and whom I highly respected as model Christians. I'd only spent time with them in a normal church setting, though, and never outside of a church sanctuary. So imagine my surprise when they began saying hurtful things to each other and threatening to storm out of the meeting. Everyone voiced their opinion, which was fine, but some of the attendees became so frustrated, they spoke loudly and in a rage. By then, my grandparents and mom had passed, so maybe this was the reason I was so deeply affected by this. The whole incident struck me in a way I wasn't prepared for, and as I drove home, I broke into tears. These were people I looked up to, and I was beyond hurt and disappointed. In the end, though, it all became a blessing in disguise, as it created a wonderful turning point for me. On my way home, I remember calling Will and sharing the meeting incident with him, and from then on, I thought a lot more about some of the things I said and did that I wouldn't want others to witness. I realized more than ever before how important it was to be the same person at all times. I learned that the way we present ourselves inside of the church is the very same way we should appear outside of it. We should work hard to do what's right, even when no one is looking. Especially since God is always looking and listening, every moment of our lives.

A SCRIPTURE TO HELP YOU

"These people honor me with their lips, but their hearts are far from me."

—MATTHEW 15:8 (NIV)

CHAPTER 3

The Golden Rule

You may or may not be able to relate to this, but there have been times when I haven't treated others the way I wanted to be treated. And I'm not proud of that. I have gossiped about people, judged them, and, worse, in my younger years, I repeated two separate things that friends shared with me in confidence. I did this once during my mid-teen years and once while I was in my late twenties. I shared their news with another friend (a different person for each incident) whom I thought *I* could share things with in confidence, too. But, needless to say, each person repeated my words to "friends" whom they believed they could confide in also. In each case, the friend who had confided in me soon discovered that I had shared what they'd told me, and while these two scenarios happened decades ago, I still think about them, and I regret betraying their trust. Sometimes I wonder if they still think about it, too, and if I could do things over, I would ... okay, so I'm just going to be blunt: I would keep my mouth shut. I would take what they told me to my grave, and I would have treated my two friends the way I want to be treated. I will say, though, that it was a great lesson learned, because ever since then, I have cherished all my friendships, and I have made a conscious effort to be the kind of friend I should be. My passion toward women—helping them, encouraging them and lifting them up—is a top priority for me, and I thank God for that.

What's really unfortunate, however, is the fact that I'd had the same thing happen to me during my teen years with two other friends—*before* I betrayed the trust of the two friends I just shared about. So, one would think that when a person knows how bad it feels to be hurt and betrayed, said person wouldn't as much as consider hurting or betraying anyone else. But this is what we do.

Women.

Men.

Human beings of all ages.

And yes, Christians, too.

Instead of treating people the way we want to be treated, we sometimes do just the opposite. Sometimes we treat them in a way that we would *never* want to be treated ourselves.

We completely ignore the Golden Rule.

We live by an ugly, selfish, tainted rule instead.

In fact, even though I learned how to be a much better friend, I still had another lesson to learn as it relates to treating people the way we want to be treated. I guess you could say I sort of flipped the script on my whole definition of friendship, because over the next twenty years, I took true sisterhood so seriously that when three friends of mine began treating me in a not-so-nice way, I saw no room for forgiveness. In each case, I was angry and then hurt and then angry and hurt all over again. My huge bag of emotions and the shock of it all affected me so greatly that I couldn't stop myself from confronting one of them by phone. I called her up, asked her about what she'd done, and when she denied it, I began telling her why I knew for sure she had. To be honest, I remember how I couldn't wait for her response, just so I could drop the bomb proof on her that I had already gathered. She, of course, didn't take that part of the conversation very well, and the next thing I knew, we began exchanging words, and she cursed me out like I was her worst enemy. We'd been great friends for many years and we sometimes saw each other weekly, so I remember hanging up on her in total shock. But, as with every relationship or disagreement, there are two sides to every story, and while I didn't say a single curse word back to her, I said several things that were likely far more hurtful—words that I knew would cut her to her core. Words she will likely never forget, and this, in and of itself, made me just as wrong.

But, as I thought back over our friendship, I realized something. This moment had been a disaster waiting to happen. The months leading up to our big blowup hadn't been good ones. Not great at all. Mostly because we'd made the mistake of mixing business with friendship—something I no longer do, because with all business dealings I pay for, my expectations are the same. I expect the same from family and friends that I would from business associates whom I have no personal relationship with. But again, it takes two, and we were both at fault in one way or another. Our friendship had also become distant and very "cordial," so unfortunately, that phone call and a couple of other unpleasant exchanges we had became a means to an end. Our friendship and sisterhood were over, and I won't deny how hurt I was. I missed all the happy times, all the fun times and long conversations we had in person and by phone. But I couldn't move beyond all that had happened or all that had been said, so when a bit of time passed and she made one last call to see if we could meet in person to fix our friendship, I never called her back. I listened to her voice message, deleted it, and went on with my life. Years later, whenever we saw each other, we would speak and hug, and I would genuinely be glad to see her, but that was pretty much it.

This is the reason that I'm not sure if confronting a friend or ghosting them is better, because with the other two friends whom I ended my friendship with, I simply stopped speaking to them. I stopped being friends with them, and they weren't even aware of it. The first of the two had always criticized me on the sly, and after years of trying to ignore it, I couldn't take it anymore. From the way one of my first apartments was decorated to a certain pair of shoes I might be wearing, she would let me know what was wrong with everything. Then, when I met and married Will, she made some dig about him being lucky to have found a woman who loves him the way I do—you know, because he was a recovering alcoholic. The day she said this, Will and I had been married for four years, and he hadn't had a drink in two of them. He has also not had a drink ever since— that was in September 1992, and he has remained sober for twenty-seven years. Note: Will does know that I'm sharing this story with you, and I must say that I have always been so very proud of him—so happy that because of God's grace, Will's desire to stop drinking, and his recovery programs, Will's life is an amazing testimony.

I also want to mention that even in those first two years of our marriage, when he did relapse, he only drank for about two weeks in each of those years. I'm not telling you this to suggest that a short relapse is any better than a long one, because it's not. I'm just pointing out that Will had already gone to inpatient treatment before I met him, so by the time we did meet, he was sober. He was in recovery and attending regular meetings. But even if he hadn't been, would that have made him any less my soulmate? Absolutely not. Will has always been the love of my life, and it is the reason that even when he did have those short relapses, I still loved him just the same. I prayed for him, supported him, and encouraged him to attend meetings as often as he needed to. I also learned as much as I could about addiction and recovery so that I could help him in any way possible.

But back to my "friend." What's interesting is that she had never been around Will when he *wasn't* sober. So her comment about him being "lucky" was something my cousin Janell would call a "punk jab." My "friend" was simply doing what she always did: criticizing me and trying to make me feel bad. Some people will do this as a way to make themselves feel better, and some will do it because they aren't happy with their own lives. But I'm sorry to say that, at the time, none of that mattered to me. I didn't care why she felt such a strong need to punk jab me repeatedly, not when I had been there for her through some of her toughest times—and unlike what I eventually did with my other friend I told you about, I didn't ask any questions. From that day on, I ghosted her. She called me a couple of days later, and I told her I was watching TV and would call her back. When I didn't, she called me the next night, and I told her again … that I was watching TV and would call her back. After that, I received no additional calls from her, and I was at peace.

This particular friend was actually the first of the three friends I ended my friendship with. So I went from ghosting her, to confronting the second friend, to ghosting the third one— who had no idea I was no longer speaking to her until she saw me in another city. Once again, my proof of betrayal wasn't just he-said, she-said evidence, it was all true. Worse, it wasn't just one incident, there were multiple offenses. This third friend, however, soon contacted me to see why I was no longer communicating with her, and I eventually shared with her why. About a year later, we also had a phone conversation, and she apologized for anything she'd done or said. By then I'd already forgiven her anyway, and I told her so. But I also knew that our friendship would likely never be the same, as way too much had happened.

Today, however, I would handle all three situations very differently. I would call each of those three friends, sit down with them face-to-face, and have a calm, heart-to-heart conversation. I would ask questions about what they'd done, allow them an opportunity to explain, and we would go from there. I would do this because everyone makes mistakes. Lord knows I have, yet some of my dearest friends have continued to love me just the same. Also, sometimes we don't see our own faults and character defects or realize that we're not being a good friend, and we need others to caringly and compassionately point this out to us. If we all did that, we could help each other grow, and we would become better women as a whole.

In the end, though, I am still here for those three ladies if they ever need me, and my greatest joy in all of this is that I no longer feel any resentment toward any of them. It took me a long time to be able to say that and truly mean it, but I have no bitterness in my heart, and I have completely forgiven them. My hope is that they have forgiven me, too, for anything I said or did to hurt them and for ending my friendships with them in an un-Christian way. My hope is that if you are currently experiencing friendship struggles, you will handle them much better than I did. If you do, you just might be able to save many of your sisterly relationships.

How we make people feel is crucial, and we should always keep that way of thinking at the forefront of our minds. We should be the best friend we can be. We should be the best family member we can be. We should love and respect everyone, regardless of who they are.

Not just *some* people, but every human being on this planet.

Why? Because we have an obligation to do what we know God wants us to do, which is to treat people the way we want to be treated.

THREE THINGS YOU CAN DO

1. Recognize when you need to correct certain behavior.

Sometimes I have realized on my own that I need to make changes. From my irritated response when receiving poor customer service (a longtime challenge of mine) to judging people without knowing their hearts or their entire story, I have known when I needed to think more positively. Or if you would ask my brothers, Willie and Michael (who are actually Junior and Mike, to my family and me), what kind of big sister I was when we were kids, they would tell you that I was *bossy*! We were adults when they shared this with me, and we all laughed about it. But it also made me think and realize the fact that I surely had been. Even today, if I think that someone whom I care about should or shouldn't be doing certain things, I will offer my opinion—sometimes when it's asked for, and sometimes when it isn't. I do it because if you ask any of my dear family members and closest friends, I want the absolute best for them. I want them all to succeed in life and be as happy as possible. But I finally learned that it is sometimes best to not say anything at all and to allow others to make whatever decisions they want to make. My job is to simply love everyone for whom they are, because they love me in the same respect. I have also met a few women along the way who tend to fall out with everyone they know very quickly. I'm talking about in only a matter of weeks or months. They also complain about everyone connected to them, or they always seem to be the victim. They have always been wronged by their spouses, children, family, friends, neighbors, church members, co-workers, supervisors, and the list goes on. I have never understood that, but my grandmother used to say, "When the same thing happens over and over, it's time to ask, 'Lord, is it me?'" My mom believed that same philosophy, and I do, too. So again, sometimes we need to evaluate *ourselves*, and at other times, we may need to have the people who love us tell us what our character defects are. Because sometimes we have no idea that they even exist, until someone brings them to our attention.

2. Know that there is a way to handle everything.

James 1:19–20 (NIV) says, "My dear brothers and sisters, take note of this: Everyone should be quick to listen, slow to speak and slow to become angry, because human anger does not produce the righteousness that God desires." It is so easy to become angry and defensive rather than staying calm and listening to what other people have to say. Especially, when we have been hurt, deceived, or betrayed. Or we decide that no one has the right to tell us anything about the way we're treating others. But keeping an open mind, realizing that we all have different opinions and mind-sets, and understanding that our way of thinking isn't the only way to think, well, this can make a beautiful difference. What we say is powerful, and we can use our words in either a positive, friendly manner or in a harsh, negative one. And if all else fails, we can always turn to God, who is our ultimate voice of reason anyhow.

3. Treat everyone the same.

This means *all* mankind. It also means eliminating any racist or discriminatory thoughts from our hearts, minds, and souls. We may not believe what some people believe, and we may not agree with certain things that some people do, but we are all God's children. All of us—sinful, flawed, and imperfect. Which is the reason that we should never spend our time focusing on what other people "used to do." Because, truth is, most of us have our own "used to do" moments that we don't want to continually be reminded of or judged for. When I was a child, my mom used to tell me this: "Don't ever think you're better than anyone, but know that you are always just as good as them." Her words have never left me, and they are truly profound. As women of God, we are obligated to love everyone. We are also obligated to forgive everyone. This can be hard (I know from past experiences), but it is certainly doable. Even if someone has physically or emotionally hurt you and you no longer want to have a relationship of any kind with them, you can still forgive them. You can still eliminate all thoughts of revenge and treat them the way you want to be treated. We can still live our lives in a way that honors God—we can live them according to Mark 11:25 (NLT), which says, "But when you are praying, first forgive anyone you are holding a grudge against, so that your Father in heaven will forgive your sins, too."

A SCRIPTURE TO HELP YOU

"In everything, therefore, treat people the same way you want them to treat you, for this is the Law and the Prophets."

—MATTHEW 7:12 (NASB)

CHAPTER 4

Losing Faith in God
and Wanting to Give Up

I will never forget the day in 1995 when my mom told me she had been diagnosed with an inoperable brain tumor that could blind her; the day in 1996 when she'd gone shopping with a friend and another vehicle slammed into them, causing my mom to hit her head against the front passenger window—and weeks later, when the doctors told us that the tumor had begun growing; the day in January 1997, the same month that my first book was officially released, when she underwent biopsy surgery; and not long after, the day we were told that while her tumor wasn't cancerous, she needed six weeks of radiation; the day in July 1998 when I drove her to the UW Hospital in Madison, Wisconsin, and we were told that her tumor was now growing toward her brain stem and that surgery would have to be performed to remove it; or the day in August 1998 when she underwent a lengthy, twelve-hour surgery.

But the most memorable day of all was in January 1999, when her neurosurgeon and radiologist jointly told her and me that they'd done all they could do for her. The reason? The first part of the tumor that they had removed the previous August was already growing back, which meant there was no need to try to remove the other section of it.

I remember feeling as though a knife had sliced my body in two. It was the most painful news I'd ever been told, and at that very moment, I began wondering how I was going to live without her. I wondered why this was happening to *my* mother, the woman who always went out of her way to do for others. The woman who always had the same smile on her face, even when she became ill.

But finally, when we left the hospital in Madison and got onto I-90 west, heading back home to Rockford, Illinois, Mom asked me to play one of her favorite gospel songs, "Lean on Me," from Kirk Franklin's album *The Nu Nation Project*. She then spoke to me in a way that she never had before. She said, "Kim, you know how people sometimes say they were so hurt that their heart felt like a hole was in it?"

"Yes," I answered.

"Well, when I am gone, you really will feel like a hole has been drilled straight through yours. And then you'll feel like the hole is so huge it can never, ever be filled up again. And after that, you'll feel even worse and like you just can't go on. But then, one day, without warning—and while I can't tell you when—you'll wake up feeling better than you did the day before. You'll smile and be happy again. You'll remember all the happy times we shared together. You'll remember everything I taught you, you'll pick up where I left off, and you'll go on to do everything I hoped and prayed for you. You'll be able to go on, because you'll know that I am in your heart always."

I remember continuing down the highway with tears flooding my face and no words to speak. I drove as best I could, barely able to see, but I decided right then and there that Mom was totally wrong about my ever being happy again. She was

wrong, and for the very first time in my life, I became angry with
God—something I never believed I would do or was capable of
doing—and my faith in Him began dwindling by the second.
I was devastated beyond devastation, and not only was I angry
with God, I was angry at the world. So much so that when my
mom and I returned home and I got her settled into our guest
bedroom, my best friend Kelli called me from Atlanta. I had
spoken to her the day before and told her that we were heading
up to the hospital in Madison for Mom's MRI—the one they
would be doing to check the area they'd removed part of the
tumor from, so that they could schedule a second surgery to
remove the remainder of it. So Kelli was calling to find out the
results, and when I told her the bad news, Kelli's immediate
response was "Well, we know God has the final say."

Now, as a Christian woman, I've heard that statement more
times than I can remember, and I certainly believe every word
of it. But on this particular day, it was the last thing I wanted
to hear. My best friend, who I've been friends with since we
were six years old, was saying something that didn't much
matter to me, and before I knew it, I heard myself saying, "I
am so sick and tired of everybody telling me what God is going
to do, when all I can see is that He's taking my mother away
from me." Of course, at that moment, the silence between
Kelli and me was deafening, and I could tell she was stunned
beyond measure. And rightfully so, because to be honest, I
had never spoken words like that to her or anyone else. I was
hurt, angry, and disappointed, and all I could think was *Here
I have been raised to love, honor, and respect* You, *God, yet
You're taking the most important person in my life? You're
taking our mother from us? My brothers and I are now going*

to be motherless? *You're taking the woman who helped every-one she could, even strangers? The woman who still tries to see the good in people who have treated her terribly? The woman who forgives people a lot quicker than most? The woman who basically only went to work, to church, and back home? The woman who thought it was important to be there for her chil-dren in every way she could and to be there for both of her parents until the day they left this earth?*

I just couldn't wrap my mind around any of what was hap-pening, and sadly, my mom slowly but surely began deteriorat-ing. In general, she was in good health, but her tumor continued to grow, and eventually, she started to experience brain swelling and had to take steroid medication, which caused all sorts of side effects. Soon, she became blind in her left eye and began having transient ischemic attacks, which were mini strokes that caused her to fall. Up until this point, she'd still been able to live alone, and she only stayed with Will and me when she wasn't feeling well or when her brain swelling was worse than usual. Sometimes she would stay for a couple of nights, and sometimes she would stay for a full week.

Of course, Will and I tried to get her to stay for as long as possible, but because my mom had always been resilient and self-sufficient, she preferred being in her own home—partly because it still gave her a certain sense of independence, and partly because I couldn't get her to see that she could *never* be a burden to us. I loved her and wanted to make her as comfortable as possible, and because she and Will had the best mother-in-law/son-in-law relationship, he would actually become upset with her when she even talked about going home, as we wanted to make sure she was safe.

But as it turned out, through the latter part of 1999, the falls became more and more frequent, so even when she was home, we didn't want her moving around too much without someone being there to walk beside her to the bathroom or to bring her what she needed. Some of my aunts and uncles would be there with her during the early daytime hours, while I was writing, and I would come in the afternoon and stay until evening, when my brother Junior arrived home from work. And I will never forget what he did for me. Because while Junior had originally held an over-the-road trucking position at the time, when I told him that I was going to begin spending the night with Mom, because I knew she preferred being at home, his response was "Look, you have a husband. So I'll come off the road and find a local position." He did this so he could be home with her every evening and overnight. That was years ago, but even now, sometimes when we're talking about Mom, I will shed tears and thank him for caring about Will and me as much as he did. I will never be able to thank him, my aunts and uncles, and my best friend Lori enough, because it really did take all of us to be there for our mom, and no one was obligated to do anything. They simply did what they did because they loved Mom, my brothers, and me so unconditionally.

There were times when Will and I could convince Mom to . spend more and more nights with us, though, and she was fine with it. Once, she even looked at me and said, "You take care of me the way I took care of my mother." Another time, she joked and said, "I guess you're the mom, and I'm the daughter now, so just tell me what you want me to do." We both laughed, and as I write this, I am reminded of how she never lost her great sense of humor. Not once.

Still, though, as much as I tried to get Mom to see that I wanted her to let me know when she needed assistance, she didn't want to bother anyone. So, in December 1999, the morning after Christmas, she fell again. Will had gone over to his youngest brother's house, and after breakfast, Mom had wanted to lie back down. I had then told her that if she needed to go to the restroom or just wanted to get up, to let me know. Our guest bedroom was right next to a bathroom, but I didn't want her taking any chances of trying to walk in there alone. However, as Will entered the house and came into the kitchen, where I was washing breakfast dishes, we both heard a loud thud and rushed through the dining room and into the hallway. What we saw was my mom lying there with her body positioned between the bedroom and bathroom doorways. She'd thought she could make it to the bathroom on her own and ... she hadn't wanted to bother me. I was always very proud of how strong, determined, and independent my mom was, as it is the reason that I am the strong, determined, independent woman I am today. But this was one time I wished my mom hadn't been any of those things.

Which is why for years, I would replay that day over and over in my mind, because this marked the beginning of more noticeable deterioration. She'd broken her ankle, we'd had to call an ambulance, and she'd spent a few days in the hospital. But, sadly, when she wasn't physically able to participate in physical therapy sessions the way her therapist needed her to, her ortho doctor told us that they needed to transfer her to a nursing facility for specialized physical rehabilitation. This was in January 2000, and when she still wasn't able to put weight on her ankle to do the exercises that the physical therapist had prescribed, her doctor called a family meeting.

For one, the high dose of steroids that my mom was taking had caused her to gain one hundred pounds, which was a hundred pounds more than she'd ever weighed in her life, so whenever she attempted to stand on her broken ankle, the pain was far too excruciating. The steroids were steadily breaking down her joints as well, and this meant that she now needed two people to turn her in bed, get her washed up, and get her dressed. Her ortho specialist and the health care team at the nursing facility informed me that she needed twenty-four-hour, full-time professional care. Her doctor also recommended that we transfer her from the physical rehabilitation floor of the facility to the general residency floor... and this was when I broke down in front of everyone. I was more devastated than I had been, because I had always told my mom that I would never place her in *any* facility. But what I found most interesting was that on one of the last couple of times I'd said that to her, many months before my mom began falling, she'd told me this: "I want you to stop saying that. We don't know how bad this is going to get, and if it has to happen, you just come and see about me." For some reason, she foresaw the extent of her illness, and her only request was that I make sure she was okay. Still, I had always ignored her comment and thought, *You're not going to a nursing facility.*

But as I sat in the meeting, trying to figure out how I could bring her home with us, her doctor said that unless I was planning to stay up twenty-four hours, every single day, a nursing facility was where my mom would receive the best care. Not to mention, she needed full-time, *skilled* care. This made me cry again, and I guess I haven't mentioned the fact that my mom was sitting in the meeting, too, and while I saw her looking at me with no particular expression, it wasn't until I wheeled her back to her room that I learned why. I told her how sorry I was, and that I didn't want her to have to be admitted there. But she looked at me and said, "Is that what you were crying about?" I told her yes, but my dear mother responded again and basically repeated her question as a statement: "I wondered what you were crying about." Then she changed the subject. It was as if she hadn't heard the same thing that the rest of us had heard in that meeting. She'd brought up a whole other conversation and hadn't seemed bothered in the least by what the doctor had said to us. Maybe because God had given her peace, and He was already preparing her for the days ahead. I don't know. But what I do know is that I had lost hope, and I was dying inside. I was feeling the kind of guilt and frustration that made me sadder than I had ever been.

Unlike mine, though, Mom's trust and faith in God were still very much intact, and over the next year and a half, every weekday (missing very few days over a twenty-two-month period), her siblings, my aunt Fannie and uncle Ben, would go to the nursing facility around six in the morning, right when the first-shift nursing assistants were getting my mom up and bathed, and they would journey with her down to the dining room for breakfast. Afterward, they would sit with her in her room for a good while longer, and many times, my dear, sweet aunt Fannie would take Mom's clothing from the dirty clothes hamper so she could wash it at home. Next, my aunt Mary Lou and uncle Charlie would arrive late morning, head down to the dining room with Mom for lunch, and then visit with her until around one o'clock. My mom usually slept for the next two to three hours (unless my uncle Cliff and aunt Vernell brought her those delicious home-cooked meals they prepared, which was something they did quite often). Then in late afternoon, I would arrive about an hour before dinner.

I do want to stop for a moment to share something else, though. I've already mentioned how I will never be able to thank my family enough for the way they helped Junior, Mike, and me take care of our mom, but for as long as I live, I will also never be able to thank my husband enough for understanding and supporting the amount of time I spent away from him during those twenty-two months. He still loved me and my mom through the entire process, and once, when I told him how sorry I was that we didn't get to spend the kind of time together that we'd become accustomed to spending and that I hoped he wasn't mad about it, he told me that if I ever apologized to him again for taking care of my mom, he really would have something to be angry about. He told me to do what I needed to do for her, and that we would eventually have our time together again. But I wasn't the only one thinking the way I was, as my mom had her own thoughts about it, too. Because what I ultimately learned from two of my aunts was that my mom had secretly been telling them to "Make Kim go home." She would then say, "Kim has a husband." So, even as ill as Mom was, she was worried about my marriage. She was concerned, but thankfully, God had given me the kind of gracious husband who understood and supported me completely.

This is the reason I smile whenever I think about another conversation Will and I had. It was one afternoon when I had spoken to my mom and her nurse, and my mom had pretty much been sleeping all day and had told her nurse that she didn't want them getting her up for dinner. So I decided that maybe I would miss going to be with her that evening, so that Will and I could go out to dinner. But after being at the restaurant for only a short while, Will noticed how distant I was. I hadn't even noticed it myself, but he looked at me and said, "I can tell right now that if you don't go to the nursing home, you're not going to be happy. So you might as well head over there as soon as we finish eating." Of course, he was right, and that's exactly what I did.

But, nonetheless, the reason I had apologized to Will was because for twenty-two months, every weekday, as soon as he arrived home from putting in long hours at work, I would spend only a few minutes with him and then be out the door. I did this because I wanted to make sure I arrived at the nursing facility before dinnertime, and then once my mom finished eating, I would sit with her, sometimes until ten or eleven at night. Sometimes I left a little earlier if she fell asleep for the evening, but I never liked leaving before then, because if she was still awake, it felt as though I was leaving her all alone. Sometimes I would cry the entire way home, because what I wanted was for my mom to be well again. I wanted things to go back to the way they were before her diagnosis. Yes, my family and I were there for her daily, and we created full-day visiting shifts, not to mention some of the beautiful third-shift nursing assistants my mom had, who would come into her room to laugh and talk with her and watch television once they finished their nightly patient rounds. This was something I had discovered one evening, when after returning home from an event I had decided to go see my mom around midnight.

Still, I wanted more for my mom. I wanted to earn the kind of money that would allow me to cover three full-time shifts of skilled nursing care so that I could bring her home. Of course, I am very grateful for the fact that my mom believed in saving for the future and that my brothers and I were able to afford one of the most reputable nursing facilities here locally, but I wanted her home. I wanted more time with my mom. I wanted many more years with her, if I could have them.

I wanted God to give me the desires of my heart.

By then, I was no longer angry with Him, though. And actually, I should clarify that my faith had returned fairly quickly, and what I hadn't known during that period was that my mom had been very much aware of my conversation with Kelli. She had been listening to every word, and a few weeks later, when she'd discovered that I was back to my old self, she'd said, "I heard you that day when you were on the phone talking to Kelli, and honey, I started praying for you right then and there. I prayed because when I am gone, God is the only One you'll have to get you through this." My mom, of course, knew that Will would be there for me, and that Junior, Mike, and I would be there for each other, along with my other family members and friends, but she also knew that only God could give me the strength, comfort, peace, and understanding I would need. So, needless to say, she'd been relieved to know that I wasn't in the same faithless, angry place I had been in before.

However, as we moved into the next year and toward her final three months or so, I began sinking into a very dark place.

And I wanted to give up.

And no one knew about it.

Not a single person, except God and me.

I didn't want to live without my mom, and as much as I love my dear Will with all my heart, I wanted to die. Through God's grace, I didn't consider taking my own life per se, but what I *did* decide was that I would continue being there for my mom until she passed. I had even prayed—many times—specifically asking God to allow me to be with her, holding her hand, when she took her last breath. After that, though, I would handle all of her arrangements exactly the way she had instructed, I would make it through her homegoing service, and then I would spend time with family members and friends who I knew would likely come to our home after the repast. Once they were gone, I would slip on my pajamas and get in bed. And never get up again. Sadly, the enemy was working overtime on me, because worse, I decided that if I simply stayed in bed and didn't eat again, this wouldn't count as taking my own life. I mentally played the whole scenario multiple times, and all I wanted was to close my eyes and never feel the gut-wrenching pain I was feeling. Ever again. My heart was broken beyond explanation, and I knew when my mom passed, the pain would become worse—and unbearable. And I didn't want to experience any of that.

But we all know how cunning the enemy is, and that he's a master at trying to trick us—especially when we are at our lowest point. He talks to us, and he's consistent about it. His job is to lie and destroy us, and when we take our focus away from God the way I was doing, we willingly invite him into our lives.

But thank God for my praying mother and everyone else who prayed for me, too, because over the next few months, as my mom continued to deteriorate and my heart remained torn in pieces, I went from asking and begging God to heal her to finally accepting the fact that she was ready to leave. She'd told me that while there had been a time when she really thought she had things right with God, it was when He'd allowed her to spend time "flat on her back" that she'd gotten things *all* the way right with Him. I mean, isn't that amazing? My mom was dying, but she was still a happy woman who inspired and encouraged everyone who came to see her. She still laughed, smiled, and joked, even though, by then, she'd lost her vision in both eyes.

But I also understood why she was ready to make her transition. Especially since she couldn't do anything for herself and her quality of life was gone. But the selfish part of me still wanted to be able to go see her daily, and I still wanted to bring her home. So I asked her, "Mom, why did this have to happen to you? And why now? When you're only fifty-seven years old?" But my mom never hesitated and said, "Even if I were eighty, you still wouldn't be ready." Then, when it dawned on me one day, too, that she was no longer able to get down on her knees to pray in the way she always had, I asked her yet another question while she was lying in bed: "Mom, you do still pray, don't you?" I wasn't sure what her response would be, but with no delay, she frowned a little, and then turned her head toward me and smiled. "Honey, yes. I never know when my Father will be coming to get me. He could come at any time."

Over these last eighteen years, I have laughed about this on many occasions, because the expression on my mom's face spoke a thousand words. She could no longer see, but she still seemed to look at me as though I had asked her the most unbelievable question ever. Then she'd quickly smiled with joy and let me know that she was waiting to go home to be with God. She sounded so happy and content about it, and this is part of the reason that John 14:1–3 (KJV) is one of my all-time favorite scriptures that I love reciting. I love all of God's Word, but these three verses give me eternal hope and the kind of beautiful peace that nothing and no one else can give: "Let not your heart be troubled: ye believe in God, believe also in me. In my Father's house are many mansions: if it were not so, I would have told you. I go to prepare a place for you. And if I go and prepare a place for you, I will come again, and receive you unto myself; that where I am, there ye may be also."

My mom knew where she was going, and she was ready.

So, finally, on November 3, 2001, two days after she had a stroke, I told her to squeeze my hand if she could hear me, and she did. I told her that she had been the best mother in the world. The kind of mother I wouldn't have even known to pray for. I told her how she'd fought a good fight, and that she didn't have to do that anymore—for me, Junior, and Mike. I told her we would be fine, and that I would always be there for both my brothers. I asked her to squeeze my hand again if she'd heard me, and she did. But this time, as she squeezed it, tears streamed down both sides of her face, and I knew she was relieved. Two of my aunts had told me that she'd been waiting for me to let her go, but it wasn't until that very moment that I realized how true this actually was. Because only minutes later, with my aunt Vernell, her sister-in-law, standing not far away from my mom's bed, my mom went home peacefully, and God answered my longtime prayer. He allowed me to be there with her, watching her take her last breath—all while holding her hand.

And my mom had been right about everything. It was God Whom I did have to turn to completely. More than I ever had in my life. My mom also used to say that for everything bad, something good comes out of it, and although I had never seen her proven wrong, I couldn't see one good thing that could possibly come from her passing. Yes, the great news was that she was finally with God and resting in peace, but besides that, I didn't see how losing her could cause anything else good to happen.

But I was very wrong about that.

I didn't realize it until many months later, but what I discovered was that my relationship with God had skyrocketed. I was closer to Him and more focused on Him than ever, and my relationship with Him has continued to grow more and more, day after day and month after month—for the last eighteen years. So, yes, I lost the woman whom I loved with all my heart, but just as she'd told me, something good certainly did come out of it. There had been a time when I had wanted to give up—and I had decided to do just that—but prayer, faith, and God's Word turned everything around for me.

Every bit of this—prayer, faith, and God's Word—can help each of us in all areas of our lives, and what I know, too, is that God doesn't place any more on us than we can bear, even when it feels like it. There is also never a reason to give up or a reason to *consider* giving up. It is true that life will never be problem-free or pain-free, but life is absolutely worth living.

Yes, when my mom was gone, I did experience every ounce of the pain she said I would feel, but today, I am happy and living my life to the fullest just as she promised. Of course, there is not a day that goes by when I don't think of her and miss her tremendously. There are still days when I lie in bed with my body curled into a ball, crying as hard as I did when she passed away. But there are far more happy days than sad ones. There are many more days when I celebrate the life my mom lived, and I try my best to make her proud. I also think about how beautiful she looked on the day of her homegoing service, as though she had never been ill a day in her life, and I know she is with me in spirit. She is with me every step of the way, as my angel in heaven, and she is forever in my heart. She is with her Heavenly Father. And that gives me peace.

THREE THINGS YOU CAN DO

1. Pray about everything.

I have always been prayerful, but it was years before I began praying every single day. It was also years before I began consciously praying about every aspect of my life. I was very good at praying multiple times per day when something went wrong or if I wanted something great to happen, but the more I grew in my faith, the more I understood how important it was to pray when things are fine—and when I don't need anything. I discovered how crucial it is to stay prayed up, so that when trouble comes (illness, death, disappointment, or heartache), you'll feel much more equipped to deal with it head-on. You won't need to turn to God at the last minute—and only because you need Him to fix something for you. If you pray regularly and consistently, you'll find yourself many steps ahead of the enemy. Yes, he will, no doubt, come for you and continue attacking you from every direction, hoping that you'll lose faith in God completely. But if you pray *daily* about everything, if you simply thank Him for all that He's done for you, life will become so much easier. If you thank God for the good times as well as the bad, you won't feel so ill-prepared when you're facing your darkest hours. You won't feel caught off guard, and you'll be ready for battle. Best of all, you'll come to understand that the bad times are what make us stronger. They force us to spend quality time with God—the kind of time we tend to take for granted when things are good—and they help us grow spiritually. They keep us from giving up.

2. Stay strong and keep going.

Just as I mentioned above, our bad times make us stronger, and they also help us appreciate our more joyous and happier times in life. And here's something else to remember, too: The struggles we experience are very necessary to get us from where we *are* to where we need to *be*. You've heard the saying "Everything happens for a reason." Well, I fully believe that. God has a plan for every human being. He doesn't purposely harm us, but He does allow certain situations to happen. We don't always understand why, of course, but the same as I couldn't understand what good could come from losing my beautiful mom, my relationship with God became my priority—just as she had hoped. My mom's illness helped her, too. Because remember when she told me that being ill had allowed her an opportunity to get things all the way right with God? And did I tell you that my brothers became much closer to Him as well? All after Mom passed away? So, staying strong, trusting God, and accepting His will is a must. Always.

3. Seek professional counseling if you need it.

I don't think I'll forget those months when I saw no other way out except giving up. I was weary and distraught, and I thought my pain was too deep to overcome—I was sure I had found an easy solution. Before my mom became ill, I never would have imagined thinking to such extremes, but as my grandmother used to say, "Honey, just keep on living." This is what she would tell me whenever I would proudly declare how I would never do *this* or I would never do *that*. And she was right. This is also the reason we have to be very careful when judging others about things we haven't experienced personally. Because until we've done so, we don't fully know what we *will* or *won't* do. Still, I didn't seek professional counseling for my grief, nor did I find a support group to attend. But looking back on things, I wish I had. Yes, prayer and my relationship with God helped me in a huge way, as did talking to others who have lost loved ones. But I believe that seeing a professional therapist and attending support group meetings would have helped me feel better a lot sooner. I know this because Will and I sat down with a counselor back in the nineties, and I was amazed at how helpful it was. This, of course, was very different from grief counseling, but my point is that counseling for any issue is well worth the time. Will and I didn't have to see our counselor for very long, yet it really helped us better understand who we were as individuals, and it brought us closer than we already were. This is something that pre-marital counseling could have assisted us with, had we taken the time to schedule it. We'd both been married before and hadn't seen a reason to spend money on a large church wedding, but we still could have scheduled sessions with our pastor or someone in private practice. God has gifted many men and women in the areas of psychology and specialized counseling (no matter what your struggle might be), and no one should ever be ashamed of seeing a therapist. Instead, we should do everything we can to get the help we need.

A SCRIPTURE TO HELP YOU

"But they that wait upon the LORD shall renew their strength; they shall mount up with wings as eagles; they shall run, and not be weary; and they shall walk, and not faint."

—ISAIAH 40:31 (KJV)

CHAPTER 5

For Everything Bad,
Something Good Comes Out of It

My mom began telling me decades ago—for everything bad, something good comes out of it—and as I previously mentioned, I have never seen her words proven wrong. It is the reason I share them with anyone who might be troubled about something, hoping they will stay encouraged. My prayer is that my mom's words will help them see—that this, too, shall pass.

There is no doubt that, for me, my mom's passing is my best example, but I also have many more instances, including my decision to take the scenic route toward finishing my degree. You see, although I was enrolled in the gifted program at my high school and graduated in 1982, at the end of my junior year, I didn't complete my bachelor's degree four years later, the way I should have. As planned, I did begin taking courses at Rock Valley College the summer after high school, and I completed the fall and spring semesters. But instead of staying at our community college for another year so I could finish my associate's degree, I decided to apply, enroll at, and attend Southern Illinois University at Carbondale. My intent had always been to transfer to a four-year university, but not until I completed two full years at Rock Valley. It's important to say, too, that during that first year, I had taken a mix of business courses and secretarial courses, based on my mom's suggestion. I'd asked her why she wanted me to take the secretarial courses, and she'd told me that it was always good to have something to fall back on. I was young and ambitious, though, and didn't really get it, so my response was "But, Mom, I'm not going to *be* a secretary. I'm going to have one." She, of course, understood my thinking and was as supportive as always, but she still said, "That's fine, but just take a few secretarial courses." So, as it turned out, I took more than a few and at the end of my freshman year, I received a one-year secretarial certificate. But nonetheless, I wanted to go away to a university sooner than planned, and I did. Of course, my parents and other family members were proud, and I couldn't have been more excited.

That is, until my parents shipped all my belongings ahead, and the two of them, my grandmother, my two brothers, and I drove eight hours, spent the night in a hotel, and got up the next morning, each of us ready for college move-in day. Actually, I was still pretty happy about all of it, but once we'd gotten everything placed in my dorm room and gone to get something to eat, reality struck me like a bulldozer. It suddenly dawned on me that my family was leaving. They were preparing to take me back to my dorm, and to my surprise, they weren't planning to park the car, get out, and stay for a while. They were simply dropping me off. And, oh, was it a disaster. I can still see myself walking up a grassy hill, falling to my hands and knees, and crying like there would be no tomorrow.

Now, though, when I think about that day, I sometimes laugh out loud, because I was a total mess. I was beyond homesick—and things never got better for me in Carbondale. That first week, I tried my best to stay focused on my studies and the degree I was working toward, but every day, I called home two to three times, and I cried myself to sleep every evening. I did this so much, that my poor roommate couldn't help regularly asking me if I was okay. I was sadder than sad, and all I wanted was to go home. But I also knew how important getting an education was, and I couldn't see leaving. Still, about two weeks after moving into my dorm, I flew home for Labor Day weekend. That Friday, I literally flew from southern Illinois to northern Illinois, but remember, at the time, this was an eight-hour drive, and I needed to get home fast. Doing so wasn't the norm, and while my parents joked about the idea of me "flying through Illinois," they were also willing to buy my plane ticket and do whatever else they had to do, if it would help me stay in school.

Which is the reason I wish I could tell you that all their great effort made a difference. I wish I could tell you that when I returned to school on Labor Day evening, my short visit home had been enough to sustain me until Thanksgiving. But I can't. What I can tell you is that, bright and early the very next day, I went over to the admissions office and withdrew from all my classes. I knew that if I wanted to receive a full refund for tuition, I had to decide what I was going to do as soon as possible. I remember one of the admissions counselors trying to talk me out of it, but my mind was made up. There was no convincing me that being homesick was only temporary, so once I signed the appropriate papers, I went back to my dorm room and called my mom—at work. I'm sure you remember my saying toward the beginning of the book that my parents worked in factories, right? So while my mom didn't have a phone sitting right next to her, I did what she'd always told me to do in case of an emergency: I dialed the number, asked for her supervisor, and then asked him if I could speak to my mom. He was a wonderfully kind man, and he never questioned why I was calling her. Probably, because over the years (especially during the summer months), I would sometimes call her just to ask her a question or to see if I could go certain places—and probably, because I had called her a lot during that whole two weeks I had been in Carbondale. My grandfather had passed away by then, but I would also call home to speak to my grandmother, as well as my dad, as he worked second shift, and then I would call home again in the evening so I could talk to my brothers once they arrived home from school—*and* so I could talk to my mom and grandmother again. I should mention, too, that long-distance phone calls were a lot more costly back in the early eighties, and at the end of my college stay (less than three weeks), my parents' phone bill was more than three hundred dollars. But again, they were trying to do all they could to keep me happy and in school. They were hoping that if I talked to my entire immediate family every single day, I would eventually call less and less. They believed I would come to love college life and that being homesick would ultimately become nothing more than a teenage memory.

But when my mom finally came to the phone that day at work, she discovered just the opposite. I told her I wanted to come home. And she told me I couldn't come home. That I needed to stay in school. That she knew it was hard being away from home, but that it would get better. Out of respect, I listened to everything she was saying, and then I dropped my explosive news. "Mom, I'm not trying to decide whether or not I'm withdrawing from school. I've already signed the papers. So I just need you and Dad to come get me."

I'm sure I don't have to tell you how hurt my mom was. She'd always had such high hopes about my education, and she'd always talked about wanting me to go farther than she had. I wanted to do that as well, but I missed my family and home far too much, and I couldn't shake it. So my dad and his friend Bob, who was more like an uncle to me, drove down to Carbondale to pick me up. But before I returned home, my mom's youngest sister, my dear, sweet aunt Ada, began checking with the community college to see if there was still time for me to enroll in fall semester classes there. Most of the courses I needed were full, though, so I went back to work part-time at Kentucky Fried Chicken, the employer I'd worked for since I was sixteen years old. Then in January, I began working full-time as a purchasing clerk for a company that manufactured cylinders—which only lasted for a few months, because by spring, I had applied to Illinois State University, and I began attending there that fall. Thankfully, this time I was only about two hours away from home, and with the exception of finals week each semester, I went home every weekend. No exaggeration. I went home every single weekend between August and May. By then, though, my parents had separated, and my dad had moved to another state, so I either took the bus or drove the car my mom had bought me that summer. Interestingly enough, my roommate and dear friend Doris was a homesick kind of girl, too, so she went home every weekend also.

As I think back, though, I know for sure that the reason my grades at ISU weren't all A's and B's was because I basically went to class during the week, did *some* studying on weekday evenings, and usually did none while I was home on the weekend. I'm not sure why this became a new way of life for me, when during my high school years homework had been so much more of a priority. In fact, there were times when I would get dropped off at our public library with two of my other dear friends, Venita and Eleanor (Neicey), just so we could study, many times staying until closing.

But by the time I entered ISU, that was no longer my frame of mind, and when my first year there ended, I came home, applied for another full-time clerical position at a different company, and began working. That was in May 1985, and sadly, that wasn't the only not-so-great decision I made. Because by June, I'd decided to get married—at twenty years old. My mom knew I wasn't ready for anything like that, and she told me so, more than once. But two months later, in August 1985, I got married anyway. I'll talk more about marriage and divorce in a later chapter, but for now, let me just say that my mom was definitely right. I wasn't ready, and neither was the man I had dated for three years.

By now, though, you may be wondering how this story relates to the topic of this chapter. You're likely wondering what good came from all the bad decisions I made back then. Well, let me tell you. For one, my grandmother passed away in March 1989, so had I gone away to a university for four years straight, right after graduating high school, I would have missed spending four of the final seven years of her life with her. I no longer lived with my mom, grandmother, and two brothers, but my apartment wasn't too far away, and I visited after work every evening, and on the weekends. I spent the kind of quality time with my mom and grandmother that I will never forget. The kind that no one else could have given me. The kind that allowed me an opportunity to laugh and talk with them and learn from them, daily and in person. Sometimes in my grandmother's bedroom with just the three of us and sometimes on the front porch of my childhood home, I spent precious time with the best women I knew—two women who possessed the kind of love, wisdom, and character that, to this day, are incomparable, irreplaceable, and priceless. My mom, my grandmother, and I were three generations of women who enjoyed an extremely close bond, and I will cherish my time with them forever.

I realize there may be a part of you that still doesn't see the good that came from delaying my college studies, but from my perspective, it was *more* than good because my mom and grandmother meant *everything* to me. Then, as it turned out, I did go on to receive my associate's degree before my grandmother passed away and my bachelor's degree about four years later. For both, I went to school in the evening, all while working full-time, yet I still reached my goal.

But here's another interesting part of the story. Remember when my mom wanted me to take secretarial courses, and I didn't think I needed them? Well, those *secretarial* courses are the reason I was qualified to work as a corporate-level secretary at two of our city's top manufacturing companies. They're the reason that one of those companies reimbursed me for all the tuition I paid out of pocket to receive my associate's degree and the other covered the tuition costs for my bachelor's. Which meant I didn't have to take out massive student loans. Then, there is the fact that I went on to become a writer who writes thousands of words in every book. And guess why I have always been able to type thousands of words so quickly? It's because of those three typing courses I took at Rock Valley College, courses I don't believe I ever would have taken had I gone straight to a four-year university and remained there all four years. I mean, don't get me wrong, getting a traditional college education is a wonderful thing, and I encourage everyone to do so, but what I'm saying, too, is that my life turned out exactly the way it was supposed to. God allowed me to follow a path that was perfect for *me*. The same as He is doing for *you*. I was able to spend some of the best times of my life with my mom and grandmother together, not knowing that I would lose my grandmother when I was only twenty-four and my mom when I was just thirty-six. I certainly had no idea that I would write even one book, let alone twenty-eight, so I will always be grateful for my mom's wisdom and advice.

And so it goes, my dear sister. For everything bad, something good always comes out of it. But if for some reason you're still thinking otherwise, let me share a few what-ifs with you.

For example, maybe you just lost your great corporate job. Or maybe it was an amazing government job that you were hoping to retire from. Well, what if God allowed this to happen so that you can finally start that business you've been wanting to launch for years? What if your business will ultimately become one of the most successful businesses in history? Because guess what? Being passed over for a promotion is what led me to discover my purpose as a writer (more on that in the next chapter). Or what if what God really wants is for you to start that women's ministry that He placed in your heart a long time ago? Because ministry doesn't always mean standing in a pulpit. Sometimes it means reaching out and helping other women who are struggling in a way you once struggled.

Or let's say your husband up and walked out on you and your children with no warning. Well, what if God allowed this to

happen for reasons you may not have considered (especially if
you chose your own husband rather than asking God to choose
your husband for you)? What if He allowed this to happen so
that He could finally introduce you to the man of your dreams?
Your true soulmate? The man who will love you more than you
ever thought possible? The man He created for you?

I could give you many more examples, but you get the picture, right? Good things always result from bad ones, even when
you're going through the worst of times. So all you have to do is
stay positive, stay in faith, and know that better days are coming. If you do this, you'll be fine. Before you know it, bad times
will become good ones, and life will go on.

Just as it should.

THREE THINGS YOU CAN DO

1. Be optimistic about everything.

This is something I've had to learn and remain conscious
of, as it is so easy to focus on the negative aspects of what
we may be going through. It's so easy to look on the dark
side of everything. But what we have to do is double our
determination and keep going. This was another piece of
wise advice that my grandmother and mom always gave me.
What we must do is face our problems and pain head-on
and push forward. We must decide and know that our trials
are only temporary. We must learn that being pessimistic
isn't good for us, and that being optimistic about everything
is what will sustain us. We must realize, too, that in many
cases, we can make a choice in terms of how we feel about
any given situation. We can choose to see the good versus

the bad. Because if we do, it will make our lives so much easier.

2. Read and meditate on specific scriptures.

As Christians, we may know many Bible verses, but there are also scriptures we don't read or hear as often as we do others. So what I do is Google scriptures relating to what I'm experiencing. When my mom passed away, I found scriptures about dealing with grief, and I came to love 2 Corinthians 5:8 (KJV) even more than I always had, which says, "We are confident, I say, and willing rather to be absent from the body, and to be present with the Lord." I thought about that scripture a lot, and I would meditate on it regularly, because it gave me peace about losing my mom. Then there is Matthew 9:22 (NLT): "Jesus turned around, and when he saw her he said, 'Daughter, be encouraged! Your faith has made you well.' And the woman was healed at that moment." Once, when I was preparing to have surgery, I called my spiritual mom, Dr. Betty Price (one of the sweetest women I know), and after she prayed with me, she told me to meditate on Matthew 9:22. I did what she advised me to do, and by the morning of my procedure, I felt a true sense of peace, and my surgery and recovery went smoothly. So, from then on, I began sharing that scripture with other women who were ill or preparing for surgery, and I still do today. And just as you can do this with grief and sickness, you can find scriptures about other things, too. Stress, decision-making, marital problems, issues with your children, problems on your job, finances, discovering your purpose, fear, anger management ... whatever your struggle is, anything at all, the Word of God can help you with it.

3. Share your testimony.

It took me years to realize that if you're not willing to talk about your own experiences, then you're also not willing to help other women who are struggling with something similar. When God delivers us from trials, heartache, and even sin, we should readily begin sharing our testimonies. We should initiate conversations with as many women as possible, because let's be honest: God doesn't allow any of us to experience pain and disappointment for no reason. So, instead of simply moving on, business as usual, we should spend lots of time rejoicing about the fact that we're now on the other side of it. We should share our stories, letting the world know just how great and amazing God truly is. So, my question for you is: Are you ashamed of your past experiences, or are you openly sharing them with the many women who could be helped by your testimony?

A SCRIPTURE TO HELP YOU

"Dear brothers and sisters, when troubles of any kind come your way, consider it an opportunity for great joy."

—JAMES 1:2 (NLT)

CHAPTER 6

The Enemy Is a Loser, and God Wins Every Single Time

Okay, so, first, let me say this: Not only is the enemy a liar, he's the biggest liar of all time. The commander of chaos. The owner of oppression. The director of deception.

His only goal in life is to destroy us.

All of us.

Every single human being.

I know I'm not telling you anything new, but with the enemy, we need to remember who and what he is, and we need to stay alert at all times. We can never underestimate his trickery or allow him to catch us at our weakest moments. When we do, we offer him an opportunity to take control. We invite him into our presence, and he begins taunting and whispering at us. He quietly and politely attacks us—although, sometimes he speaks loudly—and before long, we begin making terrible decisions.

We do his dirty work.

We go against God's will.

And then, sometimes in only a matter of seconds, the enemy does what he does best: He abandons us. He leaves us to fend for ourselves, and he moves on to his next victim. Why? Because when we willingly do his work, he no longer needs to coach us. He celebrates the fact that we've become more focused on him than we are on God, and that we have basically gifted him more time to prey on others.

Still, the enemy is no match for God. He pretends to be, but he's not. Sadly, though, he is cunning and skillful enough to make us believe his lies, and I know firsthand what he is capable of doing. There is no doubt that two of his best ways of attacking us are through illness and death, but he tries to hurt us in other ways, too. Sometimes he will simply set out to ruin our hopes and aspirations. He will block every opportunity presented to us. He will tell us that our dreams are nothing more than childlike fantasies, and that we will never see them come to pass.

This was how I began feeling while working for various employers. From the time I graduated high school, I knew I wanted to work in the business world and climb the corporate ladder. Back then, I couldn't imagine anything better, and my main goal in life was to find success in corporate America. Either that or I wanted to build a career at a state or city government agency, as long as it allowed me to work in a business-oriented capacity.

But as it turned out, between 1985 and 1996, I worked for six different employers and held *ten* different positions. I would begin each one feeling excited for maybe a few months, and then I would plan my next résumé-submitting campaign. Some jobs I held for two years and some I held for as little as four months. I would settle into each position with super high hopes, but soon I would either become bored with my job responsibilities or discover that there was no chance for further advancement—and no opportunity to earn more money.

But in the midst of that eleven-year period, the worst of the worst happened. A company I worked for passed me over for a promotion, even though I had received great performance reviews, I had been with the company for two years, and I had completed my bachelor's degree with honors. In contrast, the candidate whom they wanted to promote—a candidate who basically had been eased into the position on a temporary basis during the job application posting period—didn't have a bachelor's degree, and while she had been with the company longer than I had, she didn't have the experience I had gained with other employers. But nontheless, you know how some companies will still honor their job posting policy, even though they've already decided who they want to hire or promote? Well, I later learned that this was the case, so when the hiring manager saw my application, Human Resources placed the position on hold. I'd never heard of that happening before, but they literally told me this, and then one of the HR executives came to my current department to talk to me, explaining that a similar position would likely be opening up soon at one of their other locations. This position would have a bit more responsibility—but it still had the same pay grade as the job I had applied for, and it would also require me to drive eighty miles round-trip, each day, to a different city. This would be an offsite position, not housed at the main corporate building where I currently worked and where I wanted to remain. I even wondered why the other candidate wasn't being encouraged to apply for that particular position, too—and why I was being encouraged to leave a corporate setting and drive so far away to a satellite location. So, I decided that I wouldn't rescind my application, and instead, I waited for the company to remove the yet-to-be-explained hold status from the position I had applied for. I waited for a good while, and when Human Resources seemed to be in no hurry to do so and then the offsite position *suddenly* became available, I gave up on waiting for the position I really wanted and applied for that one.

I'm sure I don't have to tell you that I received *that* promotion with no problem at all. But, for the sake of conversation, I'm going to tell you anyway.

I got the promotion—with no problem at all.

And then, almost immediately, the corporate position was miraculously released from hold, and the other candidate was promoted into it as soon as possible. To say I was hurt and disappointed is an understatement, and my days of wearing dresses and business suits to work became near nonexistent, as I was no longer motivated in that respect. My desire to go to work on any day of the week was gone, and some mornings I felt so down and out that I had to force myself out of bed when the alarm went off. On other days, I shed many tears. I dreaded going to a place that had treated me so unfairly with no explanation, and worse, when I voiced my concerns in a meeting, asking why they'd promoted someone who didn't have better qualifications, one of the executives spoke coldly and said, "We all have choices of where we want to work."

This is certainly very true, and companies can, in fact, hire and promote whomever they want. But I naively believed that working hard, being qualified, and loving the company I worked for would be enough. Yes, during my teen years, my mom had tried to prepare me for what I might experience one day, but still, when it happened, I was heartbroken. She'd explained how there would be times when I would have to work twice as hard and be twice as qualified to be considered for certain employment opportunities, and that sometimes, not even that would be enough. She'd told me this because I was black. But what I'd learned, too, was that being black *and* being a woman sometimes made things that much more difficult. I was blessed to have a few managers and directors who saw past color and gender, and they treated me the same as they treated everyone else. But with others, not so much, and the infamous glass ceiling soon became a concrete one. Still, I always tried to do over and above what my positions called for, and I worked hard at being as professional as possible. This was something I learned from a wonderful woman named Kathy Vigna, whom I had the great privilege of working for in my early twenties.

But it was what it was. And while there is certainly more to the story, the most important part is that one day I woke up, I went to work, and I gave my two weeks' notice. I ended my employment with the company I'm speaking about, and that whole experience became life changing. That period of unfairness, which was nothing more than a bold, cruel attack from the enemy, became my new inspiration. It made me realize that I was never going to climb the corporate ladder, and best of all, it caused me to go deep in prayer. I prayed, and soon I began thinking about my purpose versus my career decisions. I thought back to my elementary, junior high, and high school teachers, and how so many of them had told me that I had a gift for writing. I then thought about some of my professors and instructors in college who had made similar comments about many of the papers I had written. Of course, later in the book I will share my writing and publishing journey in more detail, but for now, I just wanted to give you some idea of how it all began.

What's important to note here, though, is that this painful experience totally renewed my way of thinking. It made me look back over my life, and it helped me realize that the reason I had never excelled at any of the career paths I had attempted was because God had something else for me to do. This also helped me understand that when we *aren't* walking in our purpose, the work we do may seem hard. We might even dread everything relating to it, and we certainly won't enjoy the overall process. I believe, too, that the reason God allows us to become uncomfortable is so that we can grow and begin focusing on our true calling.

Interestingly enough, by the time I did begin writing my first book, I had been working a whole year in a position with the City of Rockford that I loved. Still, I knew in my heart that writing was my purpose, and that I had to keep going with it. I was excited because what the enemy had used to attack me ultimately became a wonderful blessing. Of course, there have been times when I have thought back to what happened all those years ago, but the good news is this: I am forever grateful to the people at that company who went out of their way to overlook me and my qualifications. I remember wanting that position so badly. But not getting it is what forced me to reevaluate everything. It is the reason I discovered so much more about who I am and who God wanted me to be.

This—discovering who God wanted me to be—is the reason that just two years ago, when I wanted to cancel my multi-book publishing contract and pay the advance back to my publisher, I didn't. To be honest, it wouldn't have been the best thing for Will and me financially, but Will knew how unhappy I was, and he fully supported my decision. However, not long after I began debating my options, my best friend Kelli and I had a long conversation, and she convinced me to hang in there. I also knew that I needed to finish writing the last two books of my Reverend Curtis Black series for my readers, as it wouldn't have seemed right, ending the series where it was.

But before I began talking to Will and Kelli about what I was planning to do, I became so miserable that I didn't think I could find the strength, desire, motivation, or determination to write either of those last two books. On some days, I literally walked around in tears, something no one outside of our home knew about—many times not even Will knew about it—but the one thing I kept doing daily was praying and asking God to help me. I asked Him to give me the strength, desire, motivation, and determination I just mentioned. Then, eventually, through tears, I began speaking the following words out loud: "Satan, you don't win. God wins *every* single time." I spoke these words whenever I felt defeated or when I simply didn't feel like writing, and God came through for me—just as He always does. Throughout my entire life, He has shielded me from my earthly enemies and protected me from the most dangerous enemy of all.

He has remained true to His Word.

And I so love Him for that.

He will shield and protect you, too—if you trust Him.

THREE THINGS YOU CAN DO

1. Know that we will never be problem-free.

I wish I could tell you something different, but until the moment we leave this earth, we will experience both good and bad days. Some will even be tragic, but this is our reality. It is true that, periodically, the enemy will pursue us, court us, and attack us, but with God, we can overcome any trouble that the enemy tries to cause. And although we may not understand it, God will sometimes allow the enemy to hurt us in various ways, so that He can fulfill a much greater plan. These moments can certainly be trying and painful, but if we remember that God reigns above all and that He will do what He says He will do, we will beat the enemy at his own game. If we give our problems to God, He will handle them accordingly, and they won't seem so overwhelming. We will come to realize that our problems are only temporary, and that some of our best times ever will soon transpire. Very soon indeed.

2. Remember that the enemy is no match for God.

As Christian women, many of us were taught this truth at a very young age. Because regardless of how sly, evil, and skillful the enemy might be, He will never outdo God. He will, of course, try his best to convince us otherwise, but he can never win. Not if we protect ourselves from him. Not if we let him know that we *don't* believe a word he says, and that who we *do* believe is our Heavenly Father and His Son, Jesus. We must regularly prove to him that we are filled with the Holy Spirit, and that we are #TeamGod and #TeamJesus forever.

3. Be bold in your faith.

I've already shared with you that when the enemy tries to distract me, I tell him that he doesn't win—and I tell him out loud. I also tell him that God wins every single time (my favorite words to say to him). I do this because my faith in God is no secret. I do it because I don't want the enemy to become confused about who I am or *Whose* I am. I also do it because I need him to understand that I will never, ever belong to him, and that if he chooses to keep coming for me, he's wasting his time. But most important, I do it because the more we focus on God and honor His Word, the more brutal and consistent the enemy becomes. He goes out of his way trying to win us over, so please know that spiritual warfare is *very* real. But again, the enemy is a loser, and God wins every single time. Best of all, God never fails at anything, and He always gets the glory, no matter what.

A SCRIPTURE TO HELP YOU

"For the LORD your God is the one who goes with you to fight for you against your enemies to give you victory."

—DEUTERONOMY 20:4 (NIV)

PART TWO

THE
PERSONAL
YOU

CHAPTER 7

Your Childhood Will Affect You for the Rest of Your Life

I've often wondered if my mom's experience—having two husbands walk out, causing her to become a single mother—is the reason I never felt a desire to have children. Especially since I love and cherish children so much, and I love my bonus son, Trenod, Will's and my two grandsons, and all our nieces and nephews as though they were my own. And I have always made sure they knew how much I loved them. However, from the time I was in my mid-teens, I was already telling my mom and grandmother that I was never having children. For one, I just couldn't imagine marrying a man, conceiving a child with him, and then having him desert me while I was pregnant, and two, I couldn't imagine being left alone after our children were born. I just couldn't, and as you likely concluded from Chapter 1, my mom's experience affected me so much that even though she is no longer here, I am sometimes still saddened by the hurt she endured.

It also didn't help that during my high school years, some of my classmates became pregnant, and while this may sound strange, it wasn't the idea of them being pregnant that bothered me. It was the fact that most of the young mothers I went to school with couldn't always attend football or basketball games on Friday evenings or other events. To this day, I'm not sure why that shook me the way it did, but all I remember thinking was how I didn't want that kind of responsibility. I couldn't imagine missing any school activities because of not being able to find a babysitter.

My mom and grandmother had thought my feelings about not having children were only temporary, and that I only felt that way because I was looking forward to going to college and having a successful career. They were positive that one day, I would fall in love, get married, and change my mind. Maybe because they'd both had children and they'd been great mothers. But all these years later, my mind has never changed, and I have never regretted my decision. I was so sure about the way I felt that when I realized how serious things were getting between Will and me, I sat down with him to discuss it. I wanted to let him know that if he wanted more children, things were likely not going to work out for us. But to my surprise and relief, he was content with having only one child, his son from his first marriage.

Of course, there is no doubt that some of you may be thinking that the choice I made was very selfish. I say this because over the years, I have heard many opinions, such as, "So you really don't want children? Wow, I feel really sorry for you." Then, there was that time when I was doing a radio interview during one of my book tours, and the production guy looked at me and said, "But the reason God placed women here is so they can procreate." He was referring to Genesis 1:28, which states that we are to be fruitful and multiply, and I fully understood why he felt the way he did. But I also knew that I had no desire to have my own children.

There were also times when my mom and I would be out and about, and certain women we knew would say things like, "Arletha, with as close as you and Kim are, don't you want her to give you some grandchildren?"

These comments were the most interesting of all to me, though, because whenever we heard them, my mom would respond matter-of-factly: "Please don't encourage my daughter to do something she doesn't want to do." My mom always supported me, and I always loved how she didn't mind standing up for me, too. This was likely one of the reasons that no one has ever been able to make me feel bad about my decision. Another reason is that I've always been very happy and content with my choice. Still, motherhood is a huge blessing for those who truly want to have children, and I admire mothers everywhere. I always have because being a mother requires a lot of dedication, and my mom used to say that having children was a life-long job—that even after your children became adults, you continued to worry about them. Still, my mom loved being a mom, and many times, my aunt Fannie would tell me that my mom would say, "I will lay down my life for my children." I know that to be true, because my mom made lots of sacrifices for my brothers and me, and she worried about us even when there was no cause to worry.

This is the reason I applaud all mothers, and the reason I believe that motherhood is the hardest and most important job anyone can have. But, at the same time, it just wasn't something I wanted for myself. It's something that many other women don't want, either.

And that's okay.

There were other incidents in my childhood that have affected my adult life, too. Such as when I was between the ages of six and eleven, and I was touched inappropriately by an adult male whom no one would have suspected. My mom, grandmother, and grandfather died not knowing this, but through God's grace, I don't much think about those years anymore and I have overcome them. Best of all, though, when I say I have forgiven everyone who has ever hurt or betrayed me, I truly mean it.

And what about some of my elementary school trauma? The kind of kiddie trauma that now makes me laugh? I certainly didn't think any of this was funny when it was happening, but as an adult, I actually find it amusing. Especially, when I think of the boys who teased me because I was taller than they were. One of them used to love to say, "Six-nine, ain't worth a dime!" He would then crack up laughing, but sometimes his comments made me sad—and ultimately, I became very self-conscious about my height. Of course, I was nowhere near six feet, nine inches—I'm only five feet, nine and a half inches today—but as I grew older, I didn't like being as tall as I was. It was the reason that I preferred wearing flat shoes more than I did heels. But, as always, my mom made me see the positive side of my long legs. She told me that one day I would be glad that I was tall, and that the only reason those boys were teasing me was because they wished that they were as tall as I was—or preferably much, much taller. Still, I had wished I was a bit shorter, at least for the time being, and there were times when I wouldn't sit or stand with good posture. I would sometimes slump forward or downward. I realize now how crazy that was, but it just goes to show how much the words and actions of others can and do affect you for the rest of your life.

I will say, though, that, thank God, not all childhood influ-
ences are bad, because I did adopt a lot of the good that I saw
in my mother, grandmother, and aunts, and I inherited their
strength, too. This is also the reason we have to be careful about
what we say and do in front of girls and young women, because
they do pay close attention to us.

How we carry ourselves, how we dress, how we speak, how
we handle our finances, how we treat other women, and how we
love and honor God should reflect the kind of positive image
we can be proud of. All of the above was very important to my
mom, but I won't deny that when I was young, I didn't like how
strict she was. I didn't like not being able to go places whenever
I wanted, like many of my friends. There were also times when
I wanted to wear certain clothing or hairstyles, but she wouldn't
allow me to do that, either, because she thought those styles
were too grown-looking. Then, there were those days when she
did allow me to ride my bike, go to the neighborhood park, or,
when I was older, go to our city's well-known skating rink, but
the unfortunate thing about that was that I always had to be the
first one leaving the park or skating rink to come home. As a
matter of fact, it was nothing for my mom or dad to come *inside*
the skating rink on a Saturday night, sometimes an hour before
midnight, when skating ended. I mean, back then, I was a teenager, so imagine how totally embarrassed I was.

And I may as well go ahead and be honest with you about
something else, too: I thought my mom was the meanest mother
on earth. It seemed as though most of my friends and classmates
could do whatever they wanted, while I had to stay at home—and
I wasn't happy about it. But by the time I entered my twenties,
I realized that my mom had done what all mothers should do:

protect their daughters and teach them how to have the utmost respect for themselves, so that others can respect them, too. My mom did what my grandmother did with her daughters, and before my mom passed away, I thanked her (more than once) for raising me the way she did. I thanked her for telling me that when she was supposed to be my mother, she was, and that she couldn't be my friend until I became an adult.

But here's the greatest news of all. No matter what your childhood experiences were—even if they were dreadful and horrifying—you can still be happy and live your best life today. You can choose to move beyond your past and thrive in the present. Sure, this is sometimes easier said than done, but remember earlier when I talked about getting professional help if you need it? I can't stress that enough, and if you are struggling with childhood trauma—verbal abuse, physical abuse, bullying, neglect, or anything else—pretending that it didn't happen, blaming those who caused your pain, or hoping that it will simply go away isn't the answer. Talking about it, praying about it, and moving forward is.

Most of all, know that your past doesn't define you, and that the absolute best thing you can do is forgive whomever you need to forgive. This is what worked for me, and I believe in my heart that it will work for you as well.

THREE THINGS YOU CAN DO

1. Confront your childhood trauma.

For years, I pushed my trauma to the back of my mind. It wasn't that I'd forgotten about the fact that I'd been touched inappropriately as a child, it was simply that I had also learned how to protect my emotions. Handling things in this particular way seemed so much easier, but during my midthirties, those troubling memories gradually returned, one by one. And I couldn't stop them. I thought about them for years, and so regularly, that it prompted me to write a novella entitled *A Deep Dark Secret*. The young girl I centered the story on endured much more trauma than I did, but creating her character and writing about her forced me to think about my own. This was also the year that I finally found the courage to talk about it to others, which helped me in more ways than I imagined, and it also gave other women the courage to share their stories with me and get the professional help they needed. Writing this story was truly therapeutic, and I thank God for that, but if I had it to do over again, I would have sought professional help many years before then. But again, openly talking about it to family members, friends, and my readers helped me in more ways than I could have imagined. So please confront whatever you're struggling with and talk to someone. You can start with your spouse, another family member, or a close friend, and then schedule an appointment with a counselor. Please also remember to pray for deliverance and total peace about all of it.

2. Forgive, forgive, forgive.

This is so crucial for all of us that I'm going to say those three words again. Forgive, forgive, forgive. Blaming and persecuting others may seem like the right thing to do— or it may seem like you have a right to do it—but as long as we continue doing so, we will never heal. Our pain will only become worse, and our resentment will soon begin destroying us. We will also become more and more enraged. However, if our anger ultimately turns to hate, we will only be hurting ourselves. We will suffer in agony, and we won't find true happiness. We also won't experience the kind of success we deserve. So please ask yourself, "Am I still harboring resentment toward my ex-husband or ex-boyfriend? Someone I haven't been in a relationship with for five, fifteen, or maybe twenty years? Or longer even? Am I still harboring resentment toward my parents, an ex-friend, or someone else—for something that happened many decades ago?" If so, please know that anger and hatred will cripple you faster than anything I can think of, and it is not the way God wants us to live. What He wants is for us to move past our pain and forgive unconditionally. This is exactly what I had to do myself. It wasn't easy, but it was very necessary. We must forgive, because we expect to *be* forgiven for some of the not-so-nice things we've done ourselves. We must forgive so we can be free.

3. Use your pain to help others.

In Chapter 5, I talked about sharing your testimony with others, but here I want to encourage you to delve a little deeper. For example, if you were physically abused as a child, seek out others who also experienced childhood abuse. If you were bullied by other children, connect with others who still haven't overcome being bullied. No matter what your trauma involves, share your own experience with others and offer to help them overcome it. Suggest that they see a professional counselor or help them find a local support group. Attend one or more of those support group meetings with them and make yourself available as much as possible. And if for some reason a certain type of group doesn't exist, create it. Because no matter what we experience, we are never alone in our struggles. There are always many others who can totally relate to what we've been through.

A SCRIPTURE TO HELP YOU

"Give all your worries and cares to God, for he cares about you."

—1 PETER 5:7 (NLT)

CHAPTER 8

The Comparison Game and Pretending to Be Someone You're Not

Exotic vacations, luxury homes, expensive vehicles, fine dining, five-star hotels, elegant weddings, college graduations, baby showers, birthday bashes, anniversary celebrations, music concerts, successful careers, and so much more.

Does any of this sound familiar? Do you know what I'm attempting to illustrate?

If so, then, yes, you guessed it. I'm describing each and every one of our social media timelines and what we see daily.

And let's not forget all the beautiful flowers and gifts that our dear husbands or the men we're dating have been kind enough to bless us with. I know I have certainly posted photos of flowers that Will has given me for my birthday, our anniversary, and Valentine's Day, as well as photos from some of our vacations. Not to mention the kazillion photos that I've posted from my book-signing events and speaking engagements. Many years' worth of them.

But here's the kicker: While we usually can't wait to share our happiest and most glamorous moments—those that our followers are most apt to click "like" or make a comment on—we don't tend to share the not-so-perfect aspects of our lives. I mean, do you really think I'm going to take a selfie as soon as

I get out of bed in the morning and post it for the entire world to see? A photo of my uncombed hair? Actually, the more I think about it, I don't believe I have *any* photos at all on social media where I don't have on at least a little eyeliner. And I certainly don't post any photos that make me appear much heavier than I am in person. This is so very sad, I know, but I'm just being honest. I'll tell you something else, too. If other people take unflattering photos of me and tag my Facebook timeline, I *immediately* untag myself. I do this because I learned years ago that using the "hide from timeline" feature on photos that others tag you in doesn't prevent your other Facebook friends from seeing them. But if you use the "remove tag" feature, it *does*.

So, no, as women, we don't tend to share the not-so-perfect parts of our lives. What we do is share the things we're most proud of, and this can sometimes cause others to begin coveting what they see on Facebook, Instagram, and Twitter. It can sometimes affect women so noticeably that they can't help wishing they could switch places with the women they follow—or at least sample some of those amazing lifestyles they believe everyone is living. Some studies are even reporting that social media is causing people to become depressed, all because they don't believe they're doing as well as the people they see online. What they don't consider, however, is that all human beings have good days and bad. We each have our best days and our worst.

As women . . . we have much more in common than we realize.

But the idea of comparing ourselves to others began long before social media came into existence, and it is partly the reason so many women are unhappy. It is the reason so many women live beyond their means and pretend to be someone they're not. This is also how copycatting and mimicking evolves, and I believe it happens for two reasons: One, we spend way too much time worrying about what other people think of us, and two, we're not as confident as we portray ourselves to be. I know I haven't always been completely confident in myself or in my skills and abilities, no matter how much self-esteem my mom instilled in me—yet I have always been very quick to say, "I don't care what other people think of me." But, in reality, I do care, and some of my most hurtful moments were when my mom was ill, and I gained more weight than I ever had in my life—and some people couldn't wait to let me know it. I'd actually begun gaining some weight before my mom became ill, but when you are skinny as a child and you don't gain any noticeable weight until you're somewhere in your late twenties ... well, let's just say that in my case, some folks could barely spew their cruel comments fast enough (as soon as they saw me approaching them), and they usually did it without saying as much as "Hi, Kim, how are you?" or "Hi, Kim, it's good to see you again."

There was no intro of any kind.

They simply went for the kill.

I'm sure I don't have to tell you, too, that if someone is bold enough to say the following, it's usually not a stranger—it's usually someone you've known for years: "Wow, you're definitely not trying to lose any weight, *are* you?" or "Hey, fatso," or "Boy, you've really picked up the weight, haven't you?" Of course, these comments didn't come from Will, my parents, my brothers, or my closest family members and friends, but they were made by *other* "family," "friends," and longtime acquaintances. Oh, and I would be totally remiss if I didn't tell you how the two people who were cruel enough to call me "fatso" would actually say it with an endearing tone and then laugh out loud about it.

It was almost as if they expected me to laugh right along with them. But I didn't see anything funny.

Not even a little.

Not in the least.

Not at all.

This was more than two decades ago, and even though I lost that weight in 2005 (in a later chapter, I'll tell you how I did it), I still remember what this kind of criticism felt like. Secretly, it made me compare myself to women who were smaller than me. But when I look back at that time in my life now, I realize how silly it was because all women are beautiful and more than good enough, regardless of color, size or age.

Then, there is this whole pretending-to-be-someone-you're-not philosophy. Throughout my life I have met many women who struggle in this area. If they visit someone who has a bigger home, they become ashamed of the house or apartment they currently reside in. If they learn that someone has a higher level of education, they feel uneducated. If they hear that someone has a top position at a prestigious corporation, and they don't, they feel less than. If they discover that someone earns a lot more money than they do, they feel impoverished.

And this, my dear, is the reason some women decide that pretending to be someone they're not is the only way to feel better about themselves. This is also when they might begin searching for a more glamorous home, even if they can't afford it. This is when they might begin purchasing top designer handbags—Gucci, Louis Vuitton, Hermès, and the like—instead of paying their mortgage, rent, or utility bills. This is when they might purchase a vehicle completely outside of their price range, or when they might begin lying about who they are altogether. Sometimes people will lie about every aspect of their lives, thinking that money and material possessions are what validate them—that it will encourage others to accept them, see them as equals, and even praise them in some sort of way. Some women will even stop wearing a hairstyle they've always loved, one that looks great on them, just so they can try a style that looks great on someone else—and *doesn't* look great on them. Sometimes they will bypass purchasing that one particular dress that will look fabulous on them, just so they can purchase a dress they've seen someone else wearing. Because again, they believe it will validate them in some way or make them seem as worthy as the person they're comparing themselves to.

What I wish all women knew, though, is that you should never feel less than anyone. You should never become obsessed with the idea of doing what someone else is doing or feel this desperate need to acquire all that someone else has been blessed with. Instead, you should focus on being the special woman that God created you to be—whomever that is. You should also focus on the amazing calling that God has assigned to your life—whatever that is.

I mean, if God has called you to be a paralegal, then be the *best* paralegal you can be and know that you don't have to become an attorney to be happy and successful—*unless* He has called you to become an attorney. Or maybe God has called you to become a chef. If so, then be the *best* chef you can be and know that you don't have to own the restaurant—*unless* He has called you to do so. If God has called you to be the executive director of a nonprofit organization, then be the *best* executive director you can be and know that you don't have to become a CEO in corporate America—*unless* He has called you to lead an entire company. If God has called you to be someone's employee, then be the *best* employee you can be and know that you don't have to start your own business—*unless* He has called you to do exactly that.

I could go on and on, but what I'm saying is, just be the woman God placed you on this earth to be and don't worry about anyone else. Let people be who they are, and you do the same. Because when we compare ourselves to others, we are also saying that God didn't do a great job when He formed us in our mother's womb. We're saying that He didn't know what He was doing. (Remember in the Introduction when I spoke about Jeremiah 1:5?) So make no mistake about it: God has created each and every one of us for a specific reason, and we should appreciate that. We should never try to diminish or think less of anyone He has designed—including ourselves. Because when we do, we're basically criticizing Him and stealing our own peace and contentment. Not to mention, comparing ourselves to others and pretending to be someone we're not requires way too much energy—the kind of energy we should be using elsewhere. It also goes against God's will. I'm not saying that we shouldn't be inspired and motivated by other women, because we should. And I'm certainly not saying that we shouldn't strive to be better women, educationally, financially, and career-wise, either. Because we should do that, too. But what I am saying is that we should do what we love and what we hold near and dear to our hearts. And most of all, we should pray and ask God what *He* wants us to do. Because in the end, this is what truly matters, more than anything else.

THREE THINGS YOU CAN DO

1. Self-evaluate.

As a writer, it has never been my dream or desire to write like anyone else. Not ever. But there have been times when I've read articles about various authors selling millions of copies of one book, and I have certainly thought how amazing it would be if I had that many readers myself. I have also read about authors writing debut titles that have become not just *New York Times* bestsellers but number one *New York Times* bestsellers, and I couldn't help thinking about the fact that none of my titles had ever made it past number thirteen. But then I arrived at a point in my life where I realized just how much God had really blessed me—in my life and my career—and how I had so much to be grateful for. I thought about the number of authors who would be thrilled out of this world just being able to make the list at all. I then thought about the number of writers who simply just want to have their books published. Period. So, by self-evaluating and realizing that God has always given me more than enough, I could see what was important and what wasn't. I could see that no matter what, being happy has nothing to do with other people. Being happy means being content and excited about all the wonderful blessings that God has given each of us *individually*. For example, some women don't even look forward to their birthdays, because they don't want to get older. But my mom and grandmother used to say, "If you don't turn another year, that can only mean one thing." What they meant was that we should be grateful to be alive. So, please, take some time to evaluate your thought process and recognize the *many* blessings you already have. Think about those wonderful blessings and callings that we sometimes take for granted.

2. Know that you are more than enough.

If I could scream this at the top of my lungs, over and over, I would. Because this is our truth. This describes who we are as women, regardless of who we once were in the past or who we have become today. We are always more than enough, because God says we are. Yesterday, today, and forever. Which is the reason we should never think lowly of ourselves. We should never think anyone is better than us. Remember what I mentioned toward the beginning of the book? The advice my mom gave me more than once? If not, here's what she said: "Don't ever think you're better than anyone, but know that you are always just as good as them." So I'm telling you, straight from my heart and with all the love I have in me, my dear sister, "Don't ever think you're better than anyone, but *know* that you are *always* just as good as them." Why? Because you absolutely and most definitely are. In Psalm 139:13–14 (NASB), David says it best, and these words so make me smile: "For You formed my inward parts; You wove me in my mother's womb. I will give thanks to You, for I am fearfully and wonderfully made; Wonderful are Your works, And my soul knows it very well." I mean, don't you just love that? Don't you want to feel the same as David? Beyond a shadow of a doubt? Don't you want to feel that way every waking hour of every day? Because that's what I'm choosing to do. I'm choosing to believe God, David, and my mom, and so should you. Because we are, in fact, fearfully and wonderfully made. We are just as good as anyone else. We are *more* than good enough. We are great women of God. We are blessed and highly favored a thousand times over.

3. Be you and do you.

So, there are times when I meet new women writers, both younger and older, and some will ask me a few questions and then say, "I want to be you when I grow up." Or "I'm trying to be you, so tell me how I can do that." I know these women mean well, and I am grateful to know that any part of my writing career has served as an inspiration to them. But what I want is for them to just be themselves—and understand that in order to switch places with me or to become me, they'd have to inherit every part of who I am, and not just the writing career that God has blessed me with. If they want to be me, then they'll have to lose their amazing mom the way I did. If they want to be me, they'll have to be okay with sometimes climbing into bed and curling themselves into a fetal position, weeping to no end, all because they miss their mom so terribly—even though she passed away eighteen years ago. If they want to be me, they'll have to struggle with occasional bouts of anxiety, hoping and praying that they won't have an attack at an inopportune time. Because when it happens, regardless of where they might be, they'll need to stop whatever they're doing so they can begin breathing deeply—in and out—until it passes. If they want to be me, they'll have to suffer with nightly insomnia, yet still get up the next morning, doing business as usual.

For the most part, though, I don't think many people stop to realize that no one has a perfect life or that we all have certain struggles, worries, fears, and concerns that no one else would want to experience. And this is the reason we all need to *be* us and *do* us, independently. We need to focus on the desires of our own hearts and the purpose that God has given each of us as individual women. The purpose He has given to you, and only you. Yes, it is certainly okay for women to feel inspired, motivated, and encouraged by other women, but what we also must do is discover our own unique voice, style, and way of doing whatever it is we have been created to do. That way, we won't have to compare ourselves to any other woman or pretend to be someone we're not. We can love our genuine selves the way we need to.

A SCRIPTURE TO HELP YOU

"Pay careful attention to your own work, for then you will get the satisfaction of a job well done, and you won't need to compare yourself to anyone else."

—GALATIANS 6:4 (NLT)

CHAPTER 9

Suffering in Silence—
Mentally and Emotionally

In October 2014, I rushed to the ER, scared to death I was having a heart attack. Will and one of his fishing buddies were out on a lake about an hour away from home, and with my being the I-don't-like-bothering-anyone kind of girl that I've always been ... I drove myself. Of course, I'm sure I don't have to tell you that a few family members, friends, and even one of my neighbors weren't happy to learn that I hadn't called to ask one of them to take me.

But again, I didn't want to bother anyone. Why? Because, well ... the hospital was only about twenty minutes or so away, and ... *I didn't want to bother anyone.*

Now, though, in hindsight, I do realize how dangerous and foolish my thinking was. Especially since for two weeks straight leading up to my emergency room visit, I'd been having constant heart palpitations. They'd been occurring during the day, and they sometimes awakened me at night, too. I'd also felt this odd degree of nervousness in my chest and heart area. In the past, I had experienced having a nervous stomach, but nervousness in my chest was something different. Not to mention, I was having shortness of breath for the first time in my life. These were all new symptoms that had persisted for more than a few days, yet I had basically decided to ignore them.

I had *decided* they would eventually go away—after I submitted the manuscript for the book I was working on.

That month and the month prior, I had sometimes written for ten to fourteen hours per day during the week, and on weekends, I traveled to book-signing events or speaking engagements. I was doing everything and then some, but on this particular Thursday afternoon when I felt my heart beating faster than normal and it seemed that I kept needing to catch my breath, I made a new decision. If these symptoms still hadn't disappeared by the time I finished writing the chapter I was working on, I would head to the ER. Because, you know ... I didn't want to stop writing in the *middle* of a chapter. Especially since I only had maybe another page or two to go, and because for the entire twenty-plus years I have been writing, I've almost never stopped writing on any given day unless I've written the last word of a chapter. This has always been sort of a quirky personal rule of mine. I don't prefer ending with one-half of a chapter or even three-quarters of one. What I prefer is starting with a totally new one the next morning. Or afternoon—that is, if I end up watching all two hours of one of the national morning shows ... or one or two rerun episodes of *Law & Order* or *Law & Order: SVU*.

But that's another story for another time, and what I'm sad to say is that I didn't stop writing until I *finished* my chapter. At one point, I did take a break and call Will to tell him how I was feeling, and while he suggested that I go to the emergency room, I told him I was going to run over to the dry cleaners to pick up the clothing I was taking on my trip to Maryland the next day. I was flying there on Friday to participate in the first evening of events and then serving as keynote speaker on Saturday. Will, of course, informed me that he was planning to stop by the cleaners to pick up my order on his way home, but I decided that I needed to head out to get some fresh air, and then, if my symptoms didn't go away, I would drive to the ER.

So, once I finished writing my chapter (yeah, crazy, I know), I got dressed and went to the cleaners. But during my drive, the symptoms seemed more noticeable. Then, once I arrived and went inside, my shortness of breath became worse. And it was then that I realized something was very wrong. It was then that I called Will back to let him know what was happening, and I drove myself to the hospital. But the more I drove the more I panicked, and I began hyperventilating. I also prayed, but I couldn't help worrying that I might be having a heart attack, and that thought alone should have been reason enough for me to realize that driving myself to the emergency room wasn't the best idea. I do remember Will saying he was on his way home and asking me if I was okay to drive, but based on what you've already read about me, I'm sure I don't have to tell you what my answer was.

But the way I saw it, it was going to take far too long for me to wait for Will to return from fishing or for me to find someone else, so I continued on my way. I will admit, though, that when a couple of people learned about this, they wanted to know why I hadn't just called an ambulance. This is a great question, and the good news is that I've learned my lesson. I won't ever take that kind of chance again, and I thank God for allowing me to make it to the hospital safely.

Still, by the time I walked inside, my symptoms had escalated, and this prompted the hospital staff to take me back to triage immediately. The attending nurse took my blood pressure and heart rate, which were way too high for resting range, and then she led me to a bed in an examination room. By then, my breathing had become so labored that one of the staff members hooked me up to oxygen.

This was when I became frightened, and I couldn't wait for Will to get there. I also started to worry about the speaking engagement I had contracted to do and the airfare the organization had paid for. I know work should have been the farthest thing from my mind, but deep down, I was concerned about not honoring my word. I worried about leaving the event founder and all the attendees hanging without warning.

But finally, when the ER doctor came in to see me, he told me right away that based on all the sitting for hours I had been doing for weeks and the flying I had done on weekends, he was ordering tests for both congestive heart failure and pulmonary embolism (a blood clot in the lung). This was not the news I wanted to hear, and while Will's arrival at the hospital did give me some peace, it didn't stop my mind from racing in every possible direction. *What if I have congestive heart failure? What if I'll need to take heart medication? What if I'll now be prone to having other heart conditions? Oh my, and what if I have a blood clot in my lung? What if I'll now have to be on blood thinners for the rest of my life?*

What if I can't get on that plane tomorrow morning and will have to pass on attending my speaking engagement?

Sadly, I was still thinking about my contractual obligation and telling myself that the event coordinator and the attendees might not understand. I told myself that they'd be angry and would never invite me back again. I believed this, because years before, I was in New York for a national TV show taping and my flight out that afternoon was delayed so long, it caused me to miss a bookstore event in Wisconsin. When I phoned the bookstore from LaGuardia Airport, the staff members seemed to understand, but the hosting book club didn't—and I don't believe they've spoken to me or attended my events since then. I apologized with all my heart, and I even acknowledged them in my book that was released the following year, but I never heard from them again. Still, I know I did the right thing, because even if someone refuses to accept our apology—a truly genuine apology—God will eliminate our worries and concerns and give us the peace we need.

There was also another event—a book club celebration in California—that I had to cancel a few days before it was to commence. This cancellation was all my fault, as I never should have agreed to attend, knowing that the reason I was even going to be in the area was because a church's women's ministry was bringing me there to speak at two of their events, two days in a row. I was still at a point in my career where I didn't know how to say no to book clubs, other literary organizations, or churches, but when I realized that I couldn't possibly add on a third event, I had no choice but to cancel with the book club. Thankfully, they were able to secure another author, who was kind enough to fly out for their event, but they weren't happy about my decision. And like the club in Wisconsin, they have never invited me back, either (which was my fear from the very beginning), and to this day, I still feel bad about having to cancel on both groups of women.

That's a whole other story, too, and one that doesn't have a lot to do with the topic of this chapter, but I really wanted to explain why I was just as worried about canceling my Maryland event as I was about my possible medical diagnosis. We should always keep our word, but sometimes delays, changes, and cancellations can't be helped. Still, I was more concerned about what others would think of me than I was about my health, which was plain senseless. This is so not who I am today, but it was definitely who I was back then.

It is likely who you once were or still are, too. Am I right?

And you do know that worrying about what someone else thinks of you and feeling as though you can never say no (even when you really need to) means you're suffering in silence, right?

Still, I lay on that hospital gurney, stressing about my impending results. Will and I waited for a while, and then the doctor came in to talk to us. He told us that because of all the symptoms I had, and what my lifestyle had been like over the last few weeks, he really had expected me to have congestive heart failure or a blood clot. But the good news was that I didn't have either. Needless to say, Will and I were relieved, but then the doctor went on to explain that I'd had an anxiety attack that had turned into a panic attack. Worse, he asked me flat out what it was I was doing to present the kind of vitals I had shown up with at the hospital. He wanted to know, and then he told me that if I didn't change it, I would, in fact, be back with one of the medical conditions he'd mentioned.

This scared me and made me reflect on a few things, and I agreed to see my primary care physician as soon as possible. One would think that I would have called him the next day, but I regret having to tell you that once Will and I arrived home, close to midnight, I packed my overnight bag, went to bed, and was up before dawn getting ready for the airport. Connie, my wonderful assistant at the time, wanted to know, "Do you think you should still be going?" Sadly, though, I told her I would be fine.

And thankfully, I was.

But then, you've heard the saying about God taking care of babies and fools, and let's just say, I was no baby in 2014. I was a grown woman, making reckless decisions, all so that I could satisfy everyone else. I did finally take somewhat of a step back, though, for about a year. But this was only after my primary care physician had informed me that I needed to take better care of myself. He wasn't asking me to stop writing or speaking at events, but he *was* asking me to slow things down. He wanted me to take some time off from traveling for about a year, and I did. And I felt so much better. Soon after, though, I returned to my normal grind, and I had also written two new books during my break.

I just couldn't seem to stop myself, and whenever I did say no to people—family, friends, or business associates—I always felt the need to explain to them *why* I couldn't do something they wanted me to do, *why* I couldn't read someone's book and offer a blurb or *why* I couldn't participate in someone's event. I'm better than I was, but even now, I'll still sometimes give great detail as to why I'm saying no, when I should be able to just say, "I'm sorry, but I can't." "I'm sorry, but I'll have to pass on reading your book." "I'm sorry, but I won't be able to attend your event this time around."

This continues to be easier said than done, though, because when we say no, it is sometimes very hard not to feel guilty about it. And again, the human side of who we are doesn't want anyone to be mad at us. We want everyone to like us and be happy with our decisions, even though this kind of thinking can destroy us. Even though it can cause extreme stress. My mom used to say that stress will kill you, and I believe her. So worrying about everyone else's demands, wants, and needs and not worrying about our own emotional well-being isn't good, and as women, we have to do better.

We have to stop worrying about who approves of us and who doesn't.

We must remember that God's approval is all we need anyway.

I'll tell you another way we suffer in silence, too: We hold grudges, and we refuse to forgive others. I know I've talked about this before but holding grudges and not forgiving those who have hurt us will cause more mental anguish and stress than we realize. It's just not good, and what most of us don't consider is the fact that the people who have hurt us are usually sleeping peacefully, night after night, with no worries whatsoever. In two words: They're good. They likely don't have a care in the world about what they've done to us, or they've forgotten about it altogether. They've moved on, and so should we.

And what about finding balance? This is something we all need to do, but many of us don't, because ... yes, you guessed it, we're worried about neglecting others. We're worried that if we don't give everyone else our undivided attention, they simply won't be able to go on without us. We worry that if we don't do *everything* for everyone, making sure *everyone* has every single thing they need, everything will fall apart completely.

Can you believe that we as women actually believe that?

Well, I know I have for many years. For whatever reason, I have worried about everyone close to me (something I inherited from my mom), and I have wanted to help fix anything that has gone wrong or I have even tried to prevent problems that might happen to many of the people I love. Some have asked me to help them in various ways, but with others, I have voluntarily helped them on my own. And please don't misunderstand what I'm saying. I absolutely do believe that we should help our family members, friends, and others, and I will continue to help or be a listening ear for them when they need me. But what I now realize, too, is that, as women, we need to evaluate what we're doing daily. We need to find balance as it relates to our family, friends, purpose, and our individual selves. It is true that all four areas of our lives deserve to have some of our time, but when we give 80 to 100 percent of that time to those first three areas, our emotional scales become way too unbalanced. The weight becomes unbearable, burdensome and uneven. More important, we need to stop excluding ourselves, and we need to make "me" time a bigger priority. We need to recognize when too many folks are coming at us from all different directions, yet no matter how much we make ourselves available to others, we don't usually have anyone making themselves available to us. And I don't think most family members or friends are *purposely* not being there for us. Of course, some are, but I believe the reason that most are not there for us is because we act as though we are *fine* all the time. We act as though we don't need anyone to lean on or depend on. We portray ourselves as the strong, independent women we were either raised up to be or learned how to be, and we become the primary go-to person for everyone in our lives. We invite every person we care about to come to us with every problem or issue they might be having. We welcome them with open arms, but when it becomes too heavy of a burden and we feel as though no one is there for us when we have our own problems and issues, well, we have no one to blame but ourselves. As women, we tend to feel as though we can take on the world and that nothing is too much for us to handle.

But this couldn't be farther from the truth, because every single woman on this earth has her limits. None of us is superhuman, and at some point, we all need to take a step back ... and take care of ourselves.

At some point, we need to stop smiling and pretending that all is well when in reality, what we want to do is sob uncontrollably. This actually happened to me a couple of years ago when my youngest brother, Mike, called me on the phone. All he did was ask me how I was doing, the same as always, but this time I didn't respond with words. This time, I burst into tears because of how exhausted and overwhelmed I was—and because I knew my exhaustion and busy schedule were the reason that I hadn't spoken to him, Junior, or my nieces and nephews in a while. But Mike completely understood, and he encouraged me in a way that I'm not sure he realized. He made a world of difference for me that day, and by the time we ended our call, I was in a much better place emotionally.

So again, please know that we need to make ourselves a bigger priority, and that there are times when we need to make ourselves our *top* priority, so that we can enjoy life the way God intended. This does not mean ignoring or forgetting about our spouses, children, family, friends, or the purpose God has assigned to our lives, but it does mean we should find the kind of balance that will give us the level of peace, contentment, and happiness we deserve.

I also don't want to forget to include childhood pain and trauma. I covered this in Chapter 7, but it's important for me to mention it here, too, because painful childhoods are another reason many people suffer in silence. We can try to mask our trauma and pretend that it doesn't bother us, when in truth it may be choking the life out of us. This may have been going on for years, when all we need to do is find the courage to talk to someone who cares about us and then find a professional who can help us heal. Yes, I'm repeating myself with this, too, but I can't stress enough how important it is and how much of a difference professional therapy can make for anyone who is struggling.

So, please know, my dear sister, that we don't have to suffer in silence.

We don't have to be miserable.

We *don't* have to be everything to everyone all the time.

We don't have to do any of this.

Not ever.

Unless we choose to.

THREE THINGS YOU CAN DO

1. Determine what you are struggling with most.

This is the first thing we should do, because as women, we tend to think we are doing just fine. We have no idea that something is very much wrong with us or that we're about to fall completely apart. For me, I had to sit down and rethink everything. I had to figure out what I *could* continue doing, personally and professionally, as well as what I could walk away from—or at the very least, take a break from. I had to admit to myself that I was involved in way too much, and that I needed help with the many responsibilities I had taken on without anyone asking me to. I even had to come to a point where I decide on certain days not to answer my phone, respond to any emails, or do much of anything except relax. Sometimes I lounge around in my pajamas, reading books and magazines or watching TV shows or movies—all day long. I don't leave the house, and on those days, Will is kind enough to go pick up whatever I want for lunch and dinner. Not to mention—those days are pretty much my guaranteed "cheat" days when it comes to food. But, oh, are those some of my best days ever. I enjoy them, and I don't feel guilty about shutting off the rest of the world and not doing anything productive. I enjoy just being with me, in my own home, in my own space. I do this because I've learned that the world still keeps moving right along, just the same. Everyone survives and no major catastrophes transpire simply because I've decided to put off my to-do list for another day or two. Life goes on, and ever since I announced to quite a few people (and responsibilities, too, I might add) that "Old Kim is gone," I have been happier and more relaxed than I ever thought I would be. Even my anxiety attacks have become few and far between, and I am at peace. And you already know that I recently took a year-long break from writing altogether, as well as pretty much everything work-related. I did what I needed to do—and it's time for you to do the same. Figure out what you're struggling with, and do whatever you need to do to eliminate it.

2. Talk to someone and seek professional guidance.

I don't think I will ever stop recommending professional help to those who need it, because so many women are either in denial about their mental and emotional struggles or they believe that things will ultimately get better on their own. Or, as Christians, many of us believe that as long as we pray and trust God, all will be well. This can, in fact, happen, because as we know, God can do anything. He can heal our minds and bodies and perform miracles of any kind. But just as I talked about in Chapter 4, God has gifted many men and women with knowledge and expertise in counseling. He has placed people here to serve and give us help when we need it. Because whether you're battling depression; suffering from anxiety attacks, panic attacks, or low self-esteem; or you simply don't know how to say no to family, friends, and others—and you want to do just that—a licensed professional can help you. Or maybe you're completely miserable and unhappy in your marriage, or you might even be struggling with an eating disorder, alcoholism, drug addiction, gambling addiction, sex addiction, or shopping addiction. Or maybe you're always in a hurry and don't know how to relax, or you lie awake at night worrying about things you will never be able to control. If so, seeing a counselor is one of the best things you can do for yourself. This can open many doors for you, and your darkest days can become so much brighter.

3. Make self-care your top priority.

Doing this can be tough for many of us. Mainly because, as women, our nurturing spirits cause us to put ourselves last on every list. Then, if we *do* decide to put ourselves first, we feel guilty about it. For years, this was my own struggle, but not anymore. Everything I was doing for my writing career and everyone else became far too taxing, distressing, and unmanageable, and I had to realize something very important: If I didn't take care of me the way I needed to, I wouldn't be here at all. If I hadn't taken a huge pause and rearranged my priorities, I would still be putting out fires for myself and everyone else and trying to do more than my mind and body were designed for. I would still be doing this, that, and the other and lying awake in the middle of the night, agonizing over tomorrow's to-do list. But thank God, I woke up, and even Will is happy about that—I'm sure because *I'm* now so much happier. I made lots of changes, and I made "Kim-Care" a priority—and as a result, I'm rested, energized, and living my life to the fullest. But now it's your turn. It's time for you, my dear, to set aside at least one day per week that you can devote to self-care. A day that you can reserve just for *you*. To start, maybe you could take yourself to a movie theater on the same day every week (that's what one of my beloved cousins does). Or maybe you could read an entire book every Saturday, or curl up in bed watching a good movie on Sunday, right after church. Or you could do any of this on whatever evening you choose. Or maybe you could begin scheduling a massage for yourself once every month. Or why not book a solo weekend getaway twice a year? Or you could even do what I've been trying recently: You could draw yourself a nice warm bubble bath, turn on a bit of instrumental smooth jazz with the volume turned down low, slip inside the tub, close your eyes, and relax—thinking only good thoughts or no thoughts at all. Another thing you can do is spend girl time with other women. What about scheduling a dinner date with one of your closest girlfriends every Thursday evening? Or whichever evening works best for the two of you. You could also join your church's women's ministry (or small group), a women's book club, a women's travel club, the YWCA, or other local women's organizations. The choices are infinite, and all you have to do is make *you* a much bigger priority than you are now. Begin celebrating and pampering yourself—as often as possible.

A SCRIPTURE TO HELP YOU

"Be anxious for nothing, but in everything by prayer and supplication, with thanksgiving, let your requests be made known to God; and the peace of God, which surpasses all understanding, will guard your hearts and minds through Christ Jesus."

—PHILIPPIANS 4:6–7 (NKJV)

CHAPTER 10

Taking Care of the Physical You

So, here's the thing: I love food. I mean, I really, really love delicious food, and I absolutely adore cakes, pies, and cookies. I enjoy them so much that if someone forced me to choose between eating dinner or having two or three slices of French silk pie or a slice of either red velvet or pineapple upside-down cheesecake from The Cheesecake Factory, there are times when I would certainly pass on dinner with no problem.

Okay, to be honest, there have already been times when I did choose multiple slices of pie or a huge slice of cheesecake, and I bypassed eating dinner altogether.

Why? Because it's like I said...I adore cakes, pies, and cookies, and I guess one could say that I am, hands-down, a sugar addict. I don't want to love sugar as much as I do, but this is who I have been since I was a young girl. So much so that when I was a child, my mom used to joke and say that I was going to lose all my teeth before I was thirty. And with all fairness to her thinking, if she and my grandmother and some of my other maternal family members hadn't had such strong teeth, there's a chance that most of mine would, in fact, be gone by now. I know this because Will's and my retired dentist once told me that your teeth and feet are hereditary. I'm sure, too, that this was the reason I needed to have more than one foot surgery, as did my mom and grandmother.

But as far as food and my great love for sweets, when I was in my twenties, there was a time when I loved burgers just as much as I loved dessert. And I ate them ... every ... single ... day. I would have a cheeseburger for lunch, along with fries, of course, and then once I left work, I would pick up another cheeseburger for dinner. I did this in my early twenties, and even after I married Will at the age of twenty-five, I continued my daily ritual. This certainly wasn't the kind of routine dinner selection that Will could have tolerated, but for the first few years of our marriage, he worked second shift. So, this meant, I could eat as many burgers as I wanted with no objections from anyone. Of course, there were many, many evenings when I went straight to my mom's house to have much healthier dinners with her, but again, I still ate burgers for lunch every day without fail.

I will say, though, that Will tried to warn me. He told me that if I didn't stop eating so many burgers (and start eating more fruits and vegetables), it would catch up with me. And it did. In more ways than one. Because not only did I slowly but surely begin gaining weight, but, well ... let's just say things stopped moving the way they should. My digestive system no longer seemed to work on its own, at least not without the help of laxatives, and when it did work without them, it sometimes took seven whole days to do so.

An entire week.

Seriously ... seven whole days.

Okay, so I realize that what I just told you may be too much information, but if my awful eating habit describes you in any way, I'm hoping you'll stop the madness well before I did. My hope is that you won't end up like me, struggling with IBS-C (which means that not even high-fiber foods or supplements do much to help you, and for me, they make things worse). My prayer is that you won't end up struggling and finding yourself doubled over in so much pain that you end up in the emergency room more times than you care to think about. Because sometimes my symptoms would become so intense that I wasn't able to make it through the night, and Will would end up taking me to the ER late in the evening. Or sometimes he would take me well after midnight, as I was always sure that one of my ovarian cysts was rupturing. On a few occasions this was true, but mostly my stabbing pain and debilitating discomfort were a result of my IBS-C condition.

That was years ago, but needless to say, one of the first things I had to do to minimize the number of IBS attacks I kept experiencing was to completely eliminate red meat from my diet. Then, even though my new way of eating allowed me to go months without experiencing severe pain, it wasn't until I stopped using artificial sweetener on a daily basis that my pain went away for good. Which is why, to this very day, I believe I'm allergic to at least one of them. I say this because most everyone else I know can consume drinks or eat foods with every artificial sweetener imaginable and have absolutely no problems. Yes, there are those studies and articles that warn against using artificial sweeteners of any kind, but I will admit, I do like drinking a diet soda every now and then, partly because, for whatever reason, certain classes of them don't cause issues for me, and partly because I don't think anything is overly bad when you do it in moderation. I believe this is true for cheeseburgers, too, along with any other high-fat, high-carb, or high-calorie foods that so many of us enjoy. Still, what I will tell you is that for my morning coffee, if I do decide to use something other than a bit of flavored creamer, I use stevia and monk fruit—and I have my wonderful former personal trainer (who is now one of my Pilates instructors), Keisha, to thank for that. Her nutritional suggestions changed my life, and I haven't been to the emergency room for IBS-C, an ovarian cyst rupture, or anything else since meeting her in January 2017.

But believe it or not, by the time I began struggling with my IBS-C issues, I was in my midforties and had already lost every bit of the weight I'd gained in my late twenties and thirties. Because you see, there was a time when I was nearly forty pounds heavier than I am currently. There was a time—in January 2002, to be exact—that I stepped on our bathroom scale and saw the numbers 2-0-0. I was literally two hundred pounds—for the first time in my life—and I can still remember how stunned, sad, and disappointed I was. Even though, there was no denying that during my mom's illness, I had pretty much eaten anything I wanted. Then, when she'd passed in November 2001, I had begun eating more than ever, and I'd done this for two months straight. To this day, though, some people don't believe I weighed two hundred pounds. Maybe because of my height—the same height I hadn't been too happy about as a child.

But scales don't lie.

Dress sizes, skirt sizes, and pants sizes don't lie, either. And what I can tell you is that instead of wearing the size eight that I do today, I found my fourteens nearly bursting at the seams—which meant that I desperately needed to be buying sixteens. Although, actually, I did buy a few items in size fourteen/sixteen from Lane Bryant, because somehow, the double numbers on their tags made me feel better. It's crazy, I know, but I tended to focus more on the number fourteen, when I knew good and well that I needed every inch that those fourteen/sixteens gave me.

As the months continued, however, I did lose down to the 190s and then to the 180s. But I spent the next three years fluctuating back and forth—gaining and losing and gaining and losing again—and I tried nearly every diet I could with only temporary success.

That is, until May 14, 2005, only eleven days after my fortieth birthday.

When I woke up that Saturday morning, the day seemed as normal as any. But then I strolled into the bathroom and caught a glimpse of myself in the mirror attached to my vanity. This was pretty much the daily norm for me—I would get up, use the restroom really quick, get on the scale, glance into the mirror, and head back into our bedroom. But not this day. No, this time, I stopped in my tracks and stared at my reflection in disgust. I'm not sure why, but that morning, as I gazed at my body, I saw a woman I almost didn't recognize. I saw a woman who looked tired and much older than forty.

I was so unhappy about my weight, and more important, the way I felt physically, that I immediately thought of the one thing I hadn't tried, which was Weight Watchers. I had already joined and attempted the online program, but I hadn't stuck with it. I'd failed and gained back the little bit of weight I had lost, the same as I'd done on every other diet. Still, there was something in me that morning that made me want to join the traditional Weight Watchers program. For some reason, I believed that going to actual meetings was the answer, so I went to the WW website and saw that there was a ten thirty a.m. meeting just down the street from where we live. Then, just as I have done with every idea or desire I've had, I went and told Will about it. He fully supported what I wanted to do, so then I called a good friend of mine to see if she wanted to go with me. To be honest, I was sure she would be just as excited as I was, because we've done so many other things together, but to my surprise, she listened and said, "I'm not trying anything else right now." Of course, I was a little disappointed, but I understood the way she felt, because what you have to know is that we really had tried one diet or exercise program after another. So I didn't blame her for wanting to sit this one out. Still, when I hung up, this made me rethink my decision. It made me second-guess what was in my heart, so I told Will that since I really didn't have anyone to go with me, maybe I shouldn't. But this was when Will told me something I will never forget. He said, "This isn't about anyone else. This is about you and what you feel you need to do for yourself."

So, needless to say, his words gave me the courage and confidence I needed to get showered, dressed, and on my way down the street for my first Weight Watchers experience. Once there, I walked in, signed up, did my first weigh-in, and stayed for the meeting, and what I learned right away was that Weight Watchers isn't a diet, it's a healthy lifestyle change. And that whole idea made all the difference for me. It is the reason that I began following the points system for the first few weeks but then quickly switched to their Core Plan program. This was also when I truly began seeing the weight come off every single week, and I never felt hungry on any day. It is my understanding that Weight Watchers eliminated the Core Plan years ago, but it totally changed my life and the way I think about food. That program is the reason I researched and studied everything I could about lean protein and nuts and grains, and it is the reason I began eating a lot more vegetables regularly. It is the reason I still eat that way today.

Because what I discovered was that low-fat and low-calorie meals weren't working for me the way they sometimes work for others. I realized that all the high-carb food I had been eating—breads, pasta, fried foods, fruit juices, cakes, pies, and cookies—was the reason I had gained weight in the first place and the reason I couldn't lose it. But three months after joining Weight Watchers and attending weekly meetings, I'd lost down just past the goal weight that my Weight Watchers leader had determined for me, which was 162 pounds. I began on May 14, 2005, weighing in at 181.4, and by August 3, 2005, I weighed in at 161.4. Then, the very next week, my Lifetime Membership countdown began, and I lost a few more pounds during that six-week monitoring process. I also felt more energized and healthier than I had in years, and while many of my maternal family members have been diagnosed with high blood pressure, including me, my blood pressure has registered at normal or below normal since losing those twenty pounds.

I haven't been a member of Weight Watchers for years, but what I know for sure is that the reason Weight Watchers worked so well for me was because of the group meetings I attended. For one, I knew I was going to be stepping onto the scale each week, just before the meeting started, and the thought of weighing in a pound or two less than I had the week prior kept me motivated. Sometimes I would be down multiple pounds. So, weighing in encouraged me to think before I ate anything, and it helped prevent me from slipping back to my old ways. I also still weigh myself at home every single day. Many health experts don't agree with this, as our weight does tend to fluctuate day to day because of inflammation, muscle weight (if you're toning up your muscles), and other reasons. But weighing myself every day has always worked well for me, and it keeps me very much aware of what I may need to do differently with my eating or exercising.

Of course, I wish I could tell you that over these last fourteen years, I haven't gained a single pound of my weight back, but I can't. The reason? I came to the realization that if I walked daily, on my treadmill or on the bike path, I could eat whatever I wanted and not gain weight. I learned how to *cheat* with fatty, high-calorie, high-carb foods—even processed foods—and still maintain my goal weight or less. I did this for more than a year, but soon, a pound or two crept up on me, and then another.

And another.

And a few more.

I would gain five or six pounds and lose them. I would gain six or seven pounds—and lose them—and this was also around the time I was diagnosed with IBS-C. But the two things that always got me back on track were: 1) praying and asking God to remove my desire to eat badly and 2) returning to the healthy lifestyle change I discovered through Weight Watchers. The idea of eating clean and healthy and getting the exercise I need is permanently etched inside my brain, and I try my best to live by that philosophy. Also, while it is a little-known fact, I was so elated about the wonderful way that Weight Watchers changed my life, I mailed a letter to their corporate office letting them know, and not long after, they hired me as a spokesperson. This was when I began traveling to various cities, speaking about Weight Watchers in predominantly black communities. I learned so much during those years, and again, I still live by their Core Plan philosophy.

I will admit, though, that when I recently took a year-long break from writing as well as from most speaking engagements, I became a bit too lax, and I ate whatever I wanted—and I did this all while doing no form of exercise whatsoever. But then, seven months ago, I joined a local Pilates studio, which I love, and when I realized I still had a few more pounds I wanted to lose, I started walking daily. I began getting on the treadmill or heading to the bike path on most days of the week, and not only have I returned to my ideal weight, but I feel so much better. I'm energized, and I feel good about myself when I look in the mirror. It feels great to comfortably fit in most of my clothing again.

Because listen: As much as we should always love and be happy with ourselves, no matter how much we weigh, there is nothing wrong with wanting to look good or feel good. There is nothing wrong with working as hard as we can to eat right and exercise, because being unhealthy is not okay.

Neglecting our physical well-being isn't good.

Being too exhausted to spend quality time with family and friends is unfortunate.

And destroying God's temple is *not* what He wants us to do. What He wants from all women is just the opposite.

What He wants is for us to take care of our physical bodies to the best of our abilities—remembering that we belong to Him.

And not ourselves.

THREE THINGS YOU CAN DO

1. Make a conscious healthy lifestyle change.

Whether we feel we need to lose a hundred pounds or no pounds at all, a healthy lifestyle should be a top priority for all women. And to begin, you might want to ask yourself the following questions: Are you tired all the time? Do you spend most of your day sitting down? Are you getting very little sleep? Or suffering with anxiety? Do you have high blood pressure? Diabetes? Or high cholesterol? If you answered yes to any of these, it is likely time for you to make a number of changes. I certainly don't have the perfect solution for anyone, but I can say that maintaining a healthy mind-set *seven days per week* is extremely helpful. This does not mean that you can never eat some of the not-so-healthy foods you really love, but it does mean not going overboard. The key is making sure you eat fattening, high-carb, high-calorie food only in moderation. For me, I tend to eat well Monday through Friday, and then I usually eat what I want on Saturday and Sunday. Still, I don't stuff myself on those two days, either, and my goal is to try to get in at least twenty to thirty minutes of walking on each weekend day. I still haven't consistently gotten back to this routine as much as I want, but years ago, I was always proud of the fact that I would even rise early on Sunday mornings, go downstairs to our workout room, get on the treadmill, and then shower and get ready for church. It was such a great feeling to get in my walking, seven days per week, and this was also when I felt my best physically. Something else I've had to work on, too, is drinking a lot more water, and I hope you'll do the same. There are several recommendations for daily amounts, but my goal is to at least try to drink the recommended amount we've known about for years: eight 8-ounce glasses, or approximately four 16.9-ounce bottles. Water has so many benefits, and sometimes we can easily confuse our moments of thirst with hunger—sometimes drinking enough water will allow us to determine whether we're truly hungry or not. And then, last but not least, you can search online for reputable websites and organizations that list healthy meal plans you can follow, or contact a registered dietitian or nutritionist you can consult with, either in person or via video chat. And you should always consult with your physician before making any diet or exercise changes. As for me, I drink an organic, low-carb, protein shake first thing every morning, and sometimes I'll scramble a couple of eggs and eat turkey or chicken sausage. Then, for lunch and dinner, it varies, but with the exception of the fried catfish or chicken I have from time to time, I tend to eat mainly grilled, baked, and broiled meats (fish, turkey, and chicken). I also eat most all vegetables, and I love salads. Then, as far as snacks, at the beginning of the week, I measure out a quarter cup of both walnuts and pecans, for variety, and I place them in enough Ziploc snack bags to last us for seven days. That way, Will and I can grab them from our countertop at any time. We also like eating sliced cucumbers with a bit of ranch dressing, sliced orange and yellow peppers, and string or curd cheese. Then, as I've mentioned, I basically eat what I want on Saturday and Sunday. I also enjoy and have gotten used to an intermittent fasting schedule, which means I eat for eight hours and fast for sixteen. I don't count my coffee or my low-carb organic shake into that time frame, though, and it still works very well for me. So much so that my body has become used to this particular schedule, and I don't feel nearly as hungry early or later in the day the way I used to. But again, always check with your doctor before making any changes to your eating or workout regimen.

2. Find a workout routine that you truly enjoy.

This is one of the most important aspects of becoming a healthier you, because if you don't enjoy your workout routine, you won't stick to it. For example, some workouts may seem too strenuous and overwhelming, while others may bore you straight into oblivion. Over the years, I have experienced both ends of the spectrum, but the day my former personal trainer, Keisha, suggested that I try Pilates, well, this was the best thing that could have happened for me. (You remember Keisha, right? My former trainer who gave me that great nutritional advice that ended my ER visits?) Actually, Keisha had recommended Pilates to me at least a year before I gave it a try, and as soon as I finished taking the free intro class to see if I liked it, I joined that same morning. I love doing Pilates on the reformer beds as well as the exercises that the instructors lead us through on the mat and at the barre and springboard. Like some of you ladies reading this, I've tried so many different forms of exercises I can't even remember all of them, but when you truly find something you love, you look forward to it. So now I try to do Pilates twice per week, I lift small weights at home, and I try to walk as many days as I can, because toning our muscles *and* doing some form of aerobic workout are both imperative. The good news, too, is that there are many options you can choose from, such as cardio—walking, running, cycling, swimming, martial arts, cardio dance, and jumping rope, to name a few; and muscle-toning—Pilates, weight training, resistance band training, Barre, floor exercises, and more. It will also help for you to find a great workout partner, someone who will help keep you accountable, and you can do the same for her. During the summer months, my best friend Lori and I try to meet four to five evenings per week at a local bike path. We have a set time, and even if we talk by phone that morning, we don't usually discuss it. We just know that we don't want to leave each other hanging, and we show up—whether we feel like it or not. Our walking sessions also allow us a chance to have quality girl time together, and we laugh and talk about everything imaginable the entire route. So again, please find a workout you love, both cardio and muscle-toning, and invite your mother, sister, sister-friend, neighbor, or co-worker to join you.

3. Encourage other women to take care of themselves.

Health is wealth. So once we know better and begin doing better, we should share our experiences with other women. We should check to make sure that all the women in our lives are taking the absolute best care of themselves. I haven't always felt comfortable doing this, because having certain conversations with the people you love and care about isn't always easy. But if we truly love someone, and we want them to live a healthy, happy life, we should try to help them in any way we can. We shouldn't criticize or try to force other women to make changes, but we can subtly or even silently encourage them. For example, when we go to lunch or dinner with them, we can order salads, lean protein—grilled, baked, or broiled—along with delicious vegetables. We can bypass sugary drinks of any kind, and we can chat about our daily workout routines. We can share how our new healthy lifestyle is the reason we have been able to eliminate certain medications, or the reason we feel ten to twenty years younger than we used to. Even better, we can invite our dear sisters in Christ to meet us at the gym, the bike path, or our homes, to walk or do other forms of exercise. We can help ourselves and other women all at the same time, so that we can become healthier and happier together. We should also make sure that all the women we know are getting comprehensive physical exams with bloodwork—not just every so often, but at least once *every* single year. The same goes for annual mammograms and Pap smears. Many of the official medical guidelines allow for less frequent testing, so the same as when making diet and exercise changes, please consult with your physician to see what he or she recommends. I never miss a year of getting any of the three, but unfortunately, I hear many women saying that they haven't been to the doctor in years. This is always very hard for me to believe, especially when I hear it from women who have full-coverage medical insurance. Some of these women haven't had a physical, lab work, a mammogram, or a Pap smear in a very long time, and that makes me sad. It's heartbreaking because early diagnosis for most illnesses and diseases can make all the difference in the long run. So please, see your doctor, get annual bloodwork and other testing, and make sure that other women in your life are doing the same.

A SCRIPTURE TO HELP YOU

"Or do you not know that your body is a temple of the Holy Spirit who is in you, whom you have from God, and that you are not your own?"

—1 CORINTHIANS 6:19 (NASB)

CHAPTER 11

Friends, Friendly Enemies,
and the Mean Girl Syndrome

As for me, I have had both: friends and friendly enemies. When I was a child, I was bullied by mean girls, and as an adult, I have been bullied by mean women. My most memorable childhood experience was in second grade. I was only seven years old, but the encounter was so traumatic, I still remember exactly how hurt and devastated I felt. Worse, to this day, I have no idea why these two so-called friends of mine quickly became "frenemies." I have no idea why two seven-year-old girls, both named Lisa, simply woke up one day and decided that they no longer liked me. All I know is that on whatever day that was, I went inside Henrietta Elementary School in Rockford, Illinois, and everything had changed. They were no longer speaking to me at all, and not only did I dread getting up and going to school, I was completely distraught.

Then it got worse.

Eventually they began walking close behind me and pushing me in a sneaky way. Sometimes they did this when our class was heading down to the lunchroom or to gym class, and sometimes they did it on the playground during recess. They treated me as though I were their worst enemy, and soon the crying that I secretly did at home journeyed into the classroom. I would walk in each morning, sit at my desk, and lay my head down on the top of it, weeping. I did this most every day, and not only did my second-grade teacher call my mom, she also mentioned it on my trifold report card. If you are like me and of a certain age, you can likely picture those heavier report cards that were used for elementary school grade reporting. But what I also remember is that my grades had dropped drastically that quarter—all my A's had plummeted to C's—and in the comments section, my teacher had said something to the effect of, "Kim mostly keeps her head down on her desk and cries all day." Even now, I so wish that I could find my elementary school report cards, because I would love to see those grades and be able to quote my teacher exactly. But what I can tell you is that, if for some reason I don't have her words quoted exactly, I know I am at least 99 percent correct. Because again, this was a very traumatic time in my young life, and you just don't forget those moments when other human beings have brought you to tears for days at a time.

But the good news is this: All the bullying suddenly came to a screeching halt.

Because, you see, once my mom realized that neither my teacher, the principal, those girls' parents, or anyone else seemed to be able to put a stop to what was happening to me, she showed up at my school during recess. She had confirmed the time the night before, and once I had finished lunch and made my way out to the playground, I looked across the asphalt lot and saw her sitting in her car. When she saw me, she got out, and I walked toward the wire fence that separated our playground from the street the school was located on. My mom walked across the sidewalk and onto the grass, now standing close enough to touch me through the fence, had she wanted to. But all she said was "Where are those two Lisas?" and I immediately felt just a little less scared and a little less sad. My spirits perked up a bit, and I pointed out my two bullies.

"Go ask them to come over here," my mom told me.

And I did.

I let them know that my mom wanted to talk to them, and strangely enough, they followed me back over to the wire fence, and my mom wasted no time saying her piece.

"If you two girls put your hands on my daughter again, you're going to have to answer to me. Do you understand?"

Both Lisas nodded their heads yes.

"Okay, now. Don't let her come home telling me you did."

There was total silence, and without saying anything more or as much as goodbye to even me, my mom walked away from the fence, got in her car, and left.

And it was then that one of the Lisas turned to me and said, "Why did you have to tell her that? We were planning to make up with you *today*, anyway."

Really? They were going to stop bullying me and pushing me *today*? Not the next day, the next week, or even the next month—but that very day was the day they'd planned to become friends with me again?

Whenever I think about that incident, I can't help laughing because I know they hadn't planned on any such thing. They only stopped bullying me because they were afraid of my mom. Which is the reason I wish my younger self had known that the only way to stop any bully is to stand up to them. Sadly, I hadn't found the courage, but my mom had stood up for me instead. This also wasn't the mom I had always known, as she was never confrontational with anyone, and certainly not with someone else's child, but I guess seeing your *own* child more heartbroken than you've ever seen her will motivate any mother to take action. And I'm so glad she did, because second grade became a much better time for me, and third grade was one of my favorite elementary school years of all.

Although, little did I know, a much more subtle form of bullying would rear its ugly head during my adult years. This time I found myself facing mean girls who were grown women. I wouldn't have expected it, but at the good ol' age of thirty-one, after self-publishing my first novel, I found myself in uncharted territory. An independent book distributor that had been buying and selling my books to independent bookstores had invited me down to a hugely attended women's expo in Memphis where the company was participating as a vendor. They'd purchased two hundred copies of my books, and they wanted me to sign them at their booth. Needless to say, I was excited, and Will had driven me down to Tennessee for the weekend. But when we'd arrived at the convention center, I spotted two different authors whom I admired. One wrote fiction and the other wrote motivational nonfiction. I was thrilled to know they were there, and I couldn't wait to head over to each of their tables to meet them, especially since, at that point, I still hadn't found any female writers who wanted to connect and stay in touch. But because these two writers at the expo had also published only one book each, I assumed that maybe they would be more open—even more so, once I told them how much I had enjoyed reading their books. But sadly, I was in for a rude awakening. I approached each author individually, and the response from both was the same. They spoke to me in sort of a dry tone, never asking what

I'd written or anything else. They simply said thank you but looked totally uninterested. So, as Will and I walked back to the area where I would be signing, Will couldn't help joking about it and said, "Wow, they treated you like, 'Look, you're here to sell your books and we're here to sell ours. But sweetheart, we have no interest in getting to know you.'"

We both laughed a little, and although I knew Will was trying to keep my spirits lifted, his words couldn't have been truer. These two women had looked at me as though they wondered why I had even taken the time to come introduce myself, and it was then that I began shying away from reaching out to other female authors. I became much more guarded, something I didn't seem to have to do with male authors. As a matter of fact, shortly after I self-published my first book, E. Lynn Harris and Eric Jerome Dickey became my brothers in the publishing industry, and they encouraged me and supported my writing efforts in a way that I will always be grateful for. Will and I still talk about both of them today, and while God did bless me with a number of other female writers with whom I was able to create wonderful bonds, some of whom I still enjoy connecting with now via social media and at various events, three of them have shown me a huge level of kindness and support in more ways than one: my dear, sweet friends Trisha R. Thomas, Trice Hickman-Hayes, and Marissa Monteilh. Of course, my cousin Patricia Haley-Glass loves and supports me, too, but our cousin-sister relationship far supersedes our relationship as fellow authors, as she has always been my heart and first best friend.

After that day in Memphis at the women's expo, though, I realized just how heartbreaking it is when women see other women as competition. I understood that the fear of someone possibly selling more books or possibly getting more publicity or attention was enough to make some women treat you pretty badly—and bad was how I felt.

That is, until I found a literary agent who offered to represent me, and she sold my second book to a New York publishing house. This became a wonderfully exciting time for me, and if that hadn't been enough, my agent and I learned that the company I was signing with was going to publish my book in hardcover—their first hardcover novel written by a black author. But it wasn't long before someone I knew attended an event and overheard a group of published female authors talking badly about my writing and how I didn't deserve to be that publisher's first black author to be published in hardcover. Of course, these women had no idea that someone I knew was in the room, likely because I was still very new to the industry. But guess what? Over the years, I have supported and helped three of these women in various ways and recommended their books to my own readers. As time went on and my career rose to a different level, they've also asked me to help them with various forms of marketing for their books, and I've done so without ever telling them what I knew about their conversation.

Not long after the big mean-girl powwow, though, I learned that because these women's books were being published by my first publisher as smaller-size, mass market paperback editions—and because they believed they were much better writers than me—it was their opinion that one of them should have been the first black author at the company to be published in hardcover. So I just saw their resentment as being similar to what happens when someone works in corporate America for twenty years, and the company hires someone younger—and from outside the company—whom the twenty-year employee now has to report to. It's not the same thing, but for my own peace of mind, that's what I compared my critics to, trying to understand their position, and then I moved on.

Still, I became that much more guarded, and then once I had written multiple books for a second New York publishing house and become a *New York Times* bestselling author, I faced another mean-girl debacle. It was back in 2006 at a large event in the Midwest that was attended by thousands. The organization that had brought in two other female authors, along with myself, to greet readers and sign books had also scheduled a panel for the three of us to speak on. But once we'd finished the panel session, we sat at our signing tables, which were lined up next to each other, and soon after, both authors left the area without telling me. Now, what you have to know is that these two authors had just spent the evening before laughing and talking with me at a private music concert that the organization had invited us to. They'd also been laughing and talking with me that morning, prior to our panel session, but then the atmosphere had changed drastically.

This cold-shouldered silent treatment had only occurred after most of the readers who had attended the panel session had lined up to have me sign their books and very few had purchased or brought books from home that were written by the other two authors. I personally knew how this felt, so as I signed books, I encouraged my readers to chat with them and buy their books, too. Still, the two authors weren't happy, and they left. This was something I didn't understand, because when I'd first started writing, I'd gone to many events where only a few people—or no one at all—had stood in line to buy my titles.

There were times when I would sit next to well-known authors, totally inspired and happy for them, as I watched them sign book after book. I was happy and encouraged, because it gave me hope about my own writing career.

But not everyone feels that way, and as soon as I saw them leaving without saying goodbye to me, I was hurt. Can you imagine? Even though I was a grown woman in my early forties? But I was so hurt that when I left the convention center, I went back to my hotel room and called Will in tears. This was one of the few events that year that he hadn't traveled to, and I was sobbing like a child. But Will stopped me head-on—with his usual genuine, brutal honesty, filled with the most love and support any wife could hope for. He said, "Okay, just stop. I want you to stop all of that. Because this is what we're going to do. We're not going to worry about who likes you and who doesn't. We're just going to keep doing what we've been doing and continue on."

And this, my friend, was a huge wake-up call. I had heard every word my dear husband had said to me, but I'm not sure that Will knows even today which of his words truly dried my tears. I'm not sure if he has any idea that it was one specific word. A tiny yet massive two-letter word. I'm not sure if he realizes that it was that beautiful, precious word "we" that totally brightened my spirits.

Because from the time I wrote my first book, Will has always seen my dream and vision as both of ours. He has supported me from beginning to end, and he has traveled on all twenty-seven national release tours for my twenty-seven books. This is what true ride-or-die really means, and when it is the love of your life who supports you this way, there aren't words enough to explain it.

But, once again, I became much more guarded and less trusting of certain women in the industry. Not because I didn't want to connect with them and spend time with them, but because I was through being hurt and betrayed. Of course, it did happen again, some of which I talked about in Chapter 3, but for the most part, I have taken many steps back and stayed in my own lane. What I decided was that having the three dear author friends I mentioned earlier was already a wonderful godsend. I also have my dearest friends who are my sisters of sisters outside of the industry—Patricia, Kelli, Lori, Janell, and Tasha—which means I have been blessed with more love and true friendship than I could have asked for. These five ladies have stood by me through my storms and triumphs, my sad times and my happiest days, and I can't imagine not having them in my life. I also have my six book club members of twenty years (seven if you count my best friend, Lori, who is also one of our members)—and these ladies are my sisters forever, too: Regina, Cathy, Cookie, Val, Emily, and Mattie, and the mothers of my nieces and nephews who check on me and lift me up regularly: April (my sister-in-law), Danetta, and Karen—three other women who are my sisters forever. I also have other amazing women in my life who are great friends and sisters who encourage and support me year after year, including my sisters-in-law Gloria and Tammy, as well as Venita, Gwyn, Pamela H., Eleanor, Connie, Pamela G., Janet, Shandra, Venae, Chandra, Cheryl, and Claudia. And then, of course, I have too many wonderful female cousins to name, the awesome women at my church, and a few other amazing authors and speakers whom I have met along the way. So my circle is filled with beautiful, kind, caring, genuine women who are always there for me. They support me, and they don't feel the need to become mean girls or friendly enemies. What I did was take some time to figure out who was being sincere and who wasn't. I discovered who I could talk to about my successes and failures and who I *couldn't* talk to about them, and I believe that this is the reason I no longer experience the kind of drama and hurt I once did.

Doing this made things so much easier, and while I, too, have thought that certain books could have been written better, certain songs could have been sung better, and certain movies could have been produced better—and sadly, I have sometimes negatively critiqued the creative work of other women in a private conversation—somehow when two or three or even a large group of women come together to tear down another woman on purpose because they can't understand why God is blessing that woman in a way they want to be blessed themselves, this is when I think it becomes that much more of a slap in the face. This is when it seems cold, cruel, and heartless. Because to me, women should always be happy for other women. We should always support, encourage, and uplift them at the highest levels. Especially since, as it is, we can sometimes find ourselves being torn down by some men who don't believe women should have careers, or even an opinion for that matter, so women should stand up and root for other women until the end of time. We should love and be happy for one another. We should *never* see other women as competition. We should celebrate each and every one of their accomplishments and treat them as lifetime sisters—because *here* is the unfortunate truth: *Women have it hard.* We all do in some form or fashion, or at some point in our lives—as did our mothers, their mothers, and the women before them. But if we stand together and make it a point to love each other, compliment each other, and fully have each other's back, we can build and create so much more together. We can experience greatness, both individually and collectively. We can do more than we ever thought imaginable.

We can become the amazing women that God has always wanted us to be.

Finally.

THREE THINGS YOU CAN DO

1. Build a tight circle of genuine friends.

This is a must. Build the kind of circle of friends that includes women who will drop everything for you when you need them. And if possible, make sure at least one or two of those friends have been your girls since childhood. My cousin Patricia is three years older than me, so she has been my best friend since birth. My best friend Kelli and I have been friends since first grade, and Lori has been my best friend since 1986. Actually, the reason I met Lori is because she and Kelli had recently become friends. I also have my wonderful cousin Janell, who I have been very close to since childhood, as well as, my dear daughter-in-law, Tasha. Then there are all the other women I mentioned in this chapter whom I have met along the way—women who have shown so much sisterly love and compassion toward me for many, many years. But most important, build a circle of women who want the best for you—women you can truly trust.

2. Be loyal to other women.

Being loyal to our spouses and other family members is a
given, but we should also be loyal to our sister-friends. This
is very important to me, because it is our dearest friends
who will have our backs no matter what—which means we
should show them the same courtesy. We should treat our
girls with love, honor, and respect and be there for them as
much as they are for us. We should go out of our way to help
them whenever they need us, and we should never deceive
them. We should always be happy for them and proud of
their accomplishments. We should be their loudest cheer-
leaders. I know when I hear great news about women in general, I can't wait to share that news with other women I know
personally, because when one woman wins, we all win. And
yes, while many of us have been guilty of saying things about
certain women behind their backs, it is as wrong as wrong
can be. But we don't have to continue down that ungodly
road of betrayal. It is so easy to involve ourselves in gossip—
another awful trick of the enemy—and to decide in our own
minds what other women should or shouldn't be doing. It is
very easy to judge them and decide what *we* think is best for
them. Because whether we dislike another woman's physical
appearance, some of her behaviors, or maybe even the terrible way she allows herself to be treated by men, it's not our
job to badmouth her to others. What we should do instead
is pray for her. I realize this is sometimes easier said than
done, because I have stressed my own opinions about others,
too, but with God, it is very much possible.

3. Pray for all friendly enemies, but don't let them hurt you.

As the saying goes, it is best to love some people from a distance. I wish that weren't the case, but unfortunately, this statement is very true. The reason? Not all women can be happy for you. Worse, not every woman who smiles in your face genuinely likes you, let alone has love for you, and some can cause you a mountain of pain. So please be careful. Continue to love everyone, just as God wants us to, but pray for discernment and use discretion when necessary. Ask God to separate you from women who might envy or feel jealous of you and from those who simply don't mean you well. Ask God to protect you from women who are out to deceive or betray you and to soften the hearts of those who fall into this category.

A SCRIPTURE TO HELP YOU

"It is not an enemy who taunts me—I could bear that. It is not my foes who so arrogantly insult me—I could have hidden from them. Instead, it is you—my equal, my companion and close friend."

—PSALM 55:12–13 (NLT)

CHAPTER 12

Every Woman Has a Soulmate—
Even If She Hasn't Met Him Yet

Not many people know this, but my marriage to Will is my third. Yes, it's true, before I met Will, I married the same man twice, and I'm sure your eyebrows are stretched high in the sky right now! Don't feel bad, though, because while that was more than thirty years ago and those two marriages were very short-lived, I'm still just as shocked about it as you. But here's the thing: I didn't pray and ask God to bring me my first husband, and my guess is that he didn't pray and ask God to bring him the woman he was supposed to marry, either. Worse, we received no pre-marital or Christian counseling whatsoever, and we absolutely were not ready for marriage. Not the first time or the second. This doesn't make either of us a bad person, it just means we weren't meant to be together as a couple. I know this, because I believe that everyone has a soulmate— even if you're married to someone else. There is no doubt that not everyone will agree with me on this, and some might even see this statement as being a bit controversial. But what I know, without question, is that Will is my one and only soulmate. He has been my soulmate for twenty-nine years and counting, and my prayer is that my former spouse has found his soulmate, too.

My prayer is that everyone does. Because as we all know, God is not a lover of divorce, and if you are engaged, I believe pre-marital counseling will help you determine whether you are meant to be together or not. It will also help you discover whether or not you really are marrying your soulmate.

Of course, you might be wondering how else a woman actually knows when she has found him. Well, for me, the first clue was the fact that I was more attracted to Will than I had ever been attracted to any man, and I can still remember the first time I laid eyes on him. Strangely enough, I was out one night with friends, at a bar no less, and I spotted Will all the way on the other side of the room. So I asked my friend Darryl, who was like a brother to me, if he knew him. Amazingly, he said yes, and proceeded across the floor to where Will was standing. I saw them exchange a few words, and to my shock, the next thing I knew, Darryl and Will were making their way toward me. In the past, Darryl had introduced me to a couple of his other friends, who I'd not had much chemistry with, so he was sort of at the point where he was a little tired of introducing me to men whom I just didn't connect with. So this time, he brought Will over and said, "Will, this is Kim. Kim, this is Will," and he walked away. He literally just left us standing there, and I was so embarrassed. As it was, I hadn't asked or expected Darryl to go tell Will that I wanted to know who he was or bring him over to meet me, and I certainly wasn't prepared to talk to a man I didn't know. But, mostly, I think I was feeling embarrassed because I didn't like the idea of Will knowing that I'd seen and shown interest in him first. I mean, because, well … isn't a man supposed to approach a woman before she approaches him? That's what I'd always thought, anyway. But given how things have turned out for Will and me, I now believe that if God has brought your soulmate into your presence, it doesn't matter who notices whom first.

Still, on that evening in November 1989, the same month that my biological father had passed and three months after my second divorce, Will and I stood there chatting, and all seemed well.

That is, until he told me that once the club closed, he wanted to get my phone number.

I agreed, but was he serious? Did he really think I was going to wait until two a.m. to give him my number? Why couldn't I give it to him now? Right in front of everyone? At that very moment, I couldn't help wondering what *other* woman was in the club. Possibly someone he might already be talking to or dating? Or worse, was he the kind of man who thought a woman whom he didn't know was going to leave and go home with him—at two o'clock on a Sunday morning?

Of course, Will and I both still laugh about that whole scenario now, but when the club hours ended, I politely walked right past him out the door, got into my car, and drove away. He was talking to another guy, and he didn't see me leaving—something I made sure of.

And that was that.

Or so I thought, until Will called Darryl, asking *him* for my phone number. Darryl didn't feel comfortable giving it to him, though, not when he learned that I hadn't given it to Will myself. But this didn't stop Will, and all he did was hang up and move on to plan B. He'd called my place of employment and asked to speak to me—which told me that after that short conversation we'd had on Saturday night, he'd remembered where I worked, and this was when I knew that he honestly wanted to see me again. But, because he worked second shift, and he lived only five minutes from my job, he invited me over for lunch. He did this more than once, but because I didn't understand why we couldn't just meet at a restaurant, I said no each time. I was already enjoying all our conversations and was feeling a genuine connection with him, but there was something else he'd said, too, that made me hesitant. You see, Will wasn't just looking for someone to date, he was looking to settle down. He told me flat out that he worked a lot of hours, and that while he'd dated a lot of women, this wasn't the kind of life he wanted to live anymore. Now, I will admit that these are exactly the kind of words any woman should want to hear, but with my having just gone through a second divorce, the idea of settling down again right away terrified me. I worried that we might begin moving too fast, and if things didn't work out, I'd be heading to divorce court again—and so would Will, as he'd been married twice before as well. So, the more we talked, the less I wanted us to become serious, even though I so loved everything about him. More important, I felt something with Will that I hadn't felt with any other man, and thus far, we'd only communicated via phone conversations. But once Will realized that he was doing all the calling and that we still hadn't gotten together in person, he soon stopped calling altogether. He'd been contacting me, sometimes daily, for three to four weeks, without my showing him the kind of interest he deserved, and I didn't blame him for moving on.

So, there it went. But throughout the rest of November and December, I became more and more frustrated with going out to clubs with my girlfriends and not meeting anyone I had true chemistry with. I also have never liked anything about the taste of alcoholic beverages, not even wine, and the few times when

I did buy a wine cooler in my early twenties, I would only take a few sips from it. So, clearly, I was only going there hoping to meet someone. And to be honest, I did meet a couple of guys who had great conversation, but they weren't men I could see myself being married to. Not because they weren't decent guys, but because they were not placed on this earth to be with me nor I with them. And it was after that, in January 1990, that I made some major decisions. I resumed taking college courses, and I decided that I no longer wanted to go on blind dates, or on dates of any kind for that matter. What I wanted to do was focus on completing the bachelor's degree program I had just begun as well as on my position as a caseworker for the State of Illinois. I made a pact with myself, and then I prayed, being very specific about what I wanted and needed.

I asked God to bring me a man who would love me as much as I loved him. And, of course, I also asked God to bring me the man He wanted me to be with.

And that was that.

I prayed, and from there, I went on with my life. But then on May 18, 1990, Kelli and I went out to that same little bar where I'd first met Will. What's ironic, though, is that Kelli and I rarely went out on Friday evenings, and you have to remember, Will worked second shift. So, unless we both went out on a Saturday, we had no chance of seeing each other. Not to mention, he still worked a lot of overtime, so I hadn't seen him on Saturdays, either. But, as fate would have it, on May 18, 1990, Will had taken a vacation day, and he was at the club that evening. To say I was happy to see him is an understatement, and as soon as our eyes met, I knew that our chemistry and attraction for one another were as strong as ever. So this time, when he asked me for my phone number, I couldn't wait to write it down and give it to him. This time, I wasn't afraid to enter a serious relationship, and once he'd called me that next Monday, Tuesday, and Wednesday, during his nightly lunch breaks ... and then when the automotive plant had shut down early that Thursday evening, and he'd come by my apartment ... and then after we'd spent many hours together on Friday, Saturday, Sunday ... and then went by both our moms' houses that Monday, which was Memorial Day ... well, that became the beginning of the rest of our lives. Actually, it had been that Sunday, during our ninety-minute drive to Milwaukee, that I realized I was in love with Will. We'd left early that morning so that we could spend the day shopping, eating, and strolling along the beach, and we'd played Johnny Gill's self-titled album the entire time (the cassette version that had just been released not more than a month or so before). At this point, we'd officially only been dating for four days, but I still knew that I was finally *in* love with a man who I believed was *in* love with me, and as you already know, Will and I were married four months later, in September. Things moved very quickly, but we have enjoyed each other for many years. We have certainly had our ups and downs and rough patches, but it has all been worth it, and I would marry Will again on any day, month, or year. Actually, I did sort of marry him again, four years ago, when we renewed our vows in Jamaica for our twenty-fifth anniversary.

So, yes, I do believe that every woman has a soulmate, and that marriage can bring about some of your happiest times. That is, if we pray and wait for God to bring us the man that *He* wants us to be with. Because like with all other areas of our lives, we must acknowledge and counsel with God about everything.

We must ask Him for guidance and keep Him at the forefront. I certainly haven't always done this, and it is the reason that I have made a number of mistakes and a few bad decisions. But thankfully, God has given me so much grace and mercy. He has also given me many chances to grow and get things right with Him. Many more than I deserve.

And He will do the same for you, too. So tell me: Are you currently searching for your soulmate? If so, have you prayed and asked God to bring this wonderful man into your life? Or maybe you're already dating your special someone. If this is true, then there are three things I want you to know. First, if a man truly wants to be with you, he will do whatever it takes to make you happy. Second, he will love and respect you the same as if you've already become his wife. Third, he won't date you for more than a year or two without asking you to marry him; which is why one of the worst things a woman can do is date a man for years, all the while trying to convince herself that he cares about her more than he actually does. Because believe me, men know who they want to be with. They know who they want to bring around their mothers, fathers, and other family members. They definitely know who they want to spend most of their time with, outside of church, work, and the gym. And if they're not spending it with you, they're sending you a very clear message regarding their long-term intentions.

But then, sometimes it's not about any of that. Sometimes women have very high expectations, and they want a certain type of husband.

And they ignore their Boaz.

Sometimes because *their* Boaz isn't as wealthy as Ruth's Boaz is in the Bible.

They ignore the wonderful man that God has created for them.

So, if this is you, I want you to ask yourself the following questions: Are you searching for someone with multiple degrees? Are you looking for a doctor, an attorney, or a corporate executive? If you are, there is certainly nothing wrong with that, but please don't become so set on status, educational background, or six-figure salaries that you overlook the wonderful man who collects your garbage every week. Please don't overlook the kind man who delivers your mail, the loyal guy who works for your electric company, or the thoughtful man who works full-time at one of your local fast food restaurants. I'm telling you this because Will worked in the factory at Chrysler Corporation for thirty years, and while his position didn't require him to have a degree, he retired with a full pension and some of the best health benefits available. Still, what's important, and the only thing that matters to me is this: Will has been the *best* part of my adult life for nearly three decades. He continues to love and treat me the way I want to be treated, and this is what I care about most.

This is what all women should care about.

Love, honor, compassion, and respect.

While you're dating, once you're married ... forever.

THREE THINGS YOU CAN DO

1. Ask God to bring you your soulmate.

You might not feel the need to hear this again, but it really is my most important piece of advice about dating. Pray, be specific about what you are asking for, and wait. God already knows what you need and what will be good for you, but He can also give you the desires of your heart. What He *won't* do, though, is bring into your life another woman's husband. This is something I have never understood or agreed with—the idea of dating a married man—and doing so should never be an option. All women should want something better for themselves—because they absolutely deserve better—and more important, this is certainly not the kind of relationship that God wants any of us to be in. So, again, you should pray, ask God to connect you with your soulmate, and be patient. I asked God to bring me a man who would love me as much as I love him, and not only do Will and I still love each other today, he still makes me laugh *every* single day, and we spend most of our time together. Not because we have to, but because we want to. Even when we have disagreements, we still appreciate one another, and we go out of our way to try to make each other happy. This is what I prayed for, and I'm here to tell you that prayer *does* work. God hears our requests, and all we have to do is trust Him to answer us. Then, once you meet the man you know you're going to marry, schedule pre-marital counseling, preferably with a Christian counselor, and learn everything you can about marriage and each other.

2. Don't make everything about you.

If you have a good man in your life, let him know how much you appreciate him. In the next chapter, I talk about the importance of appreciating your husband, but even while you're dating someone, this philosophy should still apply. You should also consider how the man in your life will feel about any decisions you're planning to make, and you should never criticize him. As Christian women, we should never criticize or talk down to anyone, but when it comes to the men in our lives, we should choose our words carefully, making sure that we are not purposely trying to make them feel bad about themselves. We should also never bring baggage from a previous relationship into a current one—causing the new man in your life to pay for mistakes that were made by someone from your past. Likewise, we should never pressure a man into buying things for us that he simply can't afford, including that huge engagement ring you may be envisioning. Because, to me, receiving a smaller diamond from the man of your dreams is much better than receiving a massive, multi-carat diamond from someone who might become your worst nightmare. To me, a relationship should center on love, commitment, and compassion, and not expensive jewelry. There is, of course, nothing wrong with receiving a large diamond, but please don't make that your priority.

3. **Know your worth.**

Before meeting Will, I dated a couple of guys who clearly didn't want an exclusive dating arrangement. I knew this because they mostly wanted to take me out to restaurants that weren't all that popular, or they wanted to visit me at my apartment. This also meant they were either dating other women in the area or they wanted the freedom to do so, should the opportunity arise for them. I should mention, too, that the city I was born and raised in—and still reside just outside of—isn't a metropolitan area, and a lot of people know a lot of the *same* people. So men like that need to be careful, because they don't want to get caught. These types of men want to date multiple women, all at the same time, and they are not the kind of men that any woman should waste her time with. Women should also make sure that the men they date thrive on being great providers and protectors. Because while no man needs to earn six figures to be considered a good man, he should still want to work as hard as possible and become the absolute best provider he can—for you, his children, and himself. The only exception is if he is disabled or struggling with health issues. You should also never accept even the slightest bit of physical, verbal, or emotional abuse, because once you're married, it will only escalate. So, please, *know your worth.* And if you happen to be a single mother, the man you date should treat your children just as well as he treats you. He should love and accept them, just as he loves and accepts you. Always. The man in your life should also support your dreams and your purpose and encourage you the same as you will be doing for him. So I guess what I'm saying is *know your worth,* know your children's worth, expect to be treated well, and don't ever feel the need to accept anything less.

A SCRIPTURE TO HELP YOU

"Then the Lord God said, 'It is not good for the man to be alone. I will make a helper who is just right for him.'"

—GENESIS 2:18 (NLT)

CHAPTER 13

Marriage Really
Is What You Make It

So I'm just going to say it: If you don't like Will Roby, then you've already decided that you don't like me. If you criticize or purposely offend him in any way, you are criticizing and offending me. This truth applies to everyone: family, friends, acquaintances, and strangers. Because from the very start, I took the idea of becoming one with my husband very seriously, and my feelings about that will never change.

In the previous chapter, I talked a little bit about my marriage to Will, and even more so about how we met, but there are a few other reasons that I believe our marriage has been a blessing to us for so many years. You already know that I prayed and asked God to bring me a certain kind of husband, but Will and I are also best friends. Yes, as husband and wife we are still very much attracted to each other from an intimacy standpoint, but we also talk about every topic you can think of. From day one, we have shared and discussed the good, the bad, and the ugly, the way close friends do. We have cried together during sad times, and we laugh together daily. We enjoy each other's company, and even when one of us has been out and about for an hour or two, we will call each other, mostly to talk about nothing important, during our drive home. Then, of course, when anything out of the ordinary happens, great or not so great, Will is always the first person I think to call, and he does the same with me.

But what I think makes even more of a difference is that we don't just *love* each other, we *like* each other. The latter is hugely important, because as Christian women, we tend to love everyone because God tells us to, and we want to honor Him. But it is not always easy to like certain people. Sometimes people will get married and stay married for decades, yet they haven't liked each other for years. Some married couples have never once been truly happy, but they don't always put forth any effort to make things better, either. They don't consider marital counseling—okay, I know what you may be thinking...here's that infamous word, "counseling," again. But, because counseling can truly help people, I won't ever stop suggesting it. I will always encourage *everyone* to get the help they need, so they can get to the root of their problems and enjoy a happier life. I will always recommend that all married couples do everything they can to fix their relationships. I will continue to remind them that no marriage is easy, and that it requires a lot of hard work. It calls for a huge amount of give-and-take, forgiveness, understanding, and devotion. My grandmother used to say "marriage is what you make it"; hence my inspiration for the title of this chapter. She began telling me this in my late teens, and I have never forgotten it—and I agree with her completely.

My grandmother also believed that because married couples do become one, everyone should respect that. So much so that she would proudly say, "My daughters-in-law aren't my daughters-in-law, they're just my daughters." And my mom was no different. She was kind to any of the young women that my brothers dated, and she was kind to any young man I dated also. But then, when she met Will, she took things to a whole other level. She loved Will immediately, and I will forever be grateful to my mom for welcoming my husband into our family with open arms. And even though Will is eleven years older than me and my mom was only ten years older than him, she still wanted him to call her "Mom." This is something that Will continues to joke about today, because again ... she was only ten years older than him. But she so loved him as her son, and he loved her the way a son loves his mother. They enjoyed being around each other, because my mom did what I believe all mothers should do when their children get married—know that they are not losing a child, and instead, they are gaining one. So many times, you will hear mothers telling anyone who will listen that "family comes first." "Blood is thicker than water." "He was my son long before he was her husband." "She was my daughter long before she was his wife." Sometimes you'll even hear siblings declaring, "He was my brother years before he became her husband," or "She was my sister years before she became his wife."

Of course, every one of those statements is true, and there's nothing wrong with loving your child or sibling more than life itself, but that still doesn't change one important fact: "For this reason a man shall leave his father and his mother, and be joined to his wife; and they shall become one flesh" (Genesis 2:24, NASB). This is what God wants for all marriages, and one of my best examples is of when my mom told me something that still makes me smile. It was a few months after Will and I were married, and since I was so used to seeing her on most days of the week, I would sometimes invite her to go to dinner with us, and a few other places, too. Especially since she was always inviting Will and me over for home-cooked meals that we never turned down. So I didn't see the problem.

But one day, my mom told me this: "I know how close you and I are—but Will comes even before me."

That was a very long time ago, but I still can't help thinking how big that was. My mom understood the importance of marriage, and how, with the exception of our Heavenly Father, no one should come before your husband or wife. All of Will's and my siblings understand this, too, and it is the reason that Will loves my brothers as his own brothers, and I love Will's sister and brothers as my own sister and brothers. Not as in-laws. This is also true for each of my aunts and uncles. They have always loved and treated Will as their blood nephew, and Will's aunts and uncles have always loved and treated me as their biological niece. Will's maternal grandmother, who coincidentally was born on the same month and day as my own maternal grandmother, always showed me a huge amount of love, too. And, of course, you've already read that my daughter-in-law, Tasha, is one of my closest friends. But just as I love my bonus son as my son, I love his wife as my daughter. Some of Will's and my happiest times are when Trenod and Tasha and our grandchildren, Alex and Trey, travel here for a visit, as well as when Will and I fly out to spend a few days with them. Trenod and Tasha's home is one of the few places I go where I am so relaxed that I have no desire to venture out elsewhere. But most of all, Will and I love them as one, and we respect their marriage.

There's more great advice that my mom gave me about marriage, too. Because, as ashamed as I am to say this, during our first year or so of matrimony, if Will and I had a disagreement,

I was done with him for the rest of the day. I was through, and I just didn't see any reason to talk to him. Will, on the other hand, didn't understand this kind of thinking, and I'll tell you how I first discovered that. There was one particular day when we were having a pretty heated argument, and while for the life of me I can't remember what it was about, I do remember storming out of the living room and into our bedroom. I left him standing where he was, and at twenty-five years old, I saw not a single thing wrong with doing that. I was more than fine with not speaking to him until the next day, or whenever, if that's what it took. But no more than two minutes after I'd left the room, he followed behind me. We gazed at each other in silence—I was still mad, of course. But then he said the most stunning thing: "Are we still going to the movies?"

Movies?

Was he kidding? The look on his face told me that he was dead serious. But did he actually think I still wanted to go *any-where* with him? As angry as I was, did he think I was just going to forget about our huge disagreement and pretend that all was great between us? Well, as it turned out, this was exactly what he'd thought, and he hadn't seen what the big deal was.

I still couldn't move past my anger, though, and that was that. But the next day, I told my mom about it. I just knew she'd understand where I was coming from, and that she'd also understand why I'd no longer had any desire to go to some movie theater. I was so sure she would see things my way that I finally just said, "Can you believe that, Mom? He actually asked me to go to the movies."

And while my mom wasted no time responding, she didn't say what I was expecting.

"I do believe it, and Will is right. That's how arguments should be handled between a husband and wife. Just because you disagree about something doesn't mean you no longer love each other. It doesn't mean your marriage is over. So you were wrong."

I heard what she said, but for a few minutes, I still wanted to wallow in my fury, and I definitely wanted to be right about the way I had been thinking. But I knew my mom was correct. I also couldn't deny that she'd always told me that Will and I should never go to sleep angry. She'd told me this before we were married, but I hadn't taken her words very seriously. After that particular conversation, though, Will and I never went hours without speaking. We said what we had to say, and we moved on.

But that still wasn't all in terms of the wonderful advice my mom gave me, as she also taught me about finances. Of course, not every woman reading this will want to hear it, and many will disagree entirely with what I'm about to share. But my mom's advice is the reason that Will and I have always been able to take care of ourselves, pay our bills on time, and save for emergencies.

My mini finance lessons first began when I was a little girl. Each Saturday morning, whenever my mom wasn't working overtime, she would sit at our dining room table writing out money orders. This took place back in the seventies, which was quite a few years before she finally decided to open a checking account. She and my dad always had more than one savings account, but for some reason, they hadn't seen a reason to spend time balancing a checkbook. Anyway, my mom would pay bills, and I would sit adjacent to her, watching. Then, as I got a little

older, maybe around ten or eleven, I would look at certain statements and ask her why she was paying them when the due date
was maybe two to three weeks down the road. This was when
she told me, "A bill is always due, so instead of waiting for a due
date, it's best to pay your bills when you receive them. That way,
you'll always be a little ahead, and you'll have less of a chance
of getting behind."

What's most interesting to me about all of this, though, is
that while my mom was the kind of mother who believed that a
child should stay in a child's place and not be involved in "grown
folks' business," she saw nothing wrong with teaching me about
finances at an early age. She made sure I knew very early in
life how important it was to have good credit, and ... okay, so
here's the part that you might not agree with, but what she told
me was that one of the best things a husband and wife can do is
keep their money together. My mom did have a separate savings
account at her company's credit union, and my dad had one at
his, but the majority of their combined income was deposited
into one primary account every Friday. After that, my mom paid
any bills that had arrived over the past week, she bought gro-
ceries, she kept out enough money to pay their tithes and offer-
ings on Sunday, and the rest remained in savings. That is, with
the exception of what she and my dad kept for spending money
and lunch money for my brothers and me before they deposited their weekly checks. They handled their finances this way
because when all money belongs to both spouses, no one ever
has to struggle unnecessarily. If my mom's car needed repair-
ing, she never had to depend on just her income to get it fixed,
and then take the chance of maybe not having enough money to
take her to her next pay period. If my dad found himself facing

some sort of emergency expense, he never had to worry about spending every dime of his money, either. Or if they needed to withdraw the money from savings, they were able to withdraw it from everything they'd saved together, regardless of how much each of them had contributed. Because again, all their money belonged to both of them, and everything was paid from one account. Actually, my mom's theory on marital finances reminds me of Ecclesiastes 4:9–11 (NIV), which says: "Two are better than one, because they have a good return for their labor: If either of them falls down, one can help the other up. But pity anyone who falls and has no one to help them up. Also, if two lie down together, they will keep warm. But how can one keep warm alone?"

Now, I will admit that if one spouse spends a lot more than the other or withdraws money that the other spouse doesn't know about—or they spend money that the budget doesn't allow for—then this arrangement can become difficult and cause major resentment. But for Will and me, it has worked for our entire marriage, and the reason Will has always encouraged me to manage our budget and bills is because of the way I was handling my own when we met. We also never make major purchases without the other person knowing about it, and this really helps a lot, too. Yes, there have been times when we have not agreed on certain purchases, and I have also sometimes been overly cautious about spending money on anything. Of course, we've had years, too, when we could have saved more money than we did. But, for the most part, my mom's philosophy has worked very well, and even today, Will and I still have joint accounts. We still deposit our incomes together, and we have no complaints.

I guess, though, as I prepare to close, that what I mostly want you to remember are my grandmother's words: "Marriage is what you make it." I want you to think about them and begin applying them to your own marriage, because no marriage is perfect. Why? Because none of us are perfect human beings. We're blemished and scarred.

We're flawed, and the men we marry are flawed.

Which is the reason we must work on ourselves individually, keep God at the center of our marriage, and then work together as a couple. We must remember 1 Corinthians 13:7 (NLT), which says, "Love never gives up, never loses faith, is always hopeful, and endures through every circumstance."

We must continue to grow in God and give our marriages the attention they deserve.

For better or worse.

For richer or poorer.

In sickness and in health.

Until death do us part.

THREE THINGS YOU CAN DO

1. Truly become one.

Will and I take this to heart, and it does not diminish the love we have for our family and friends. It just means that we choose to stand together as husband and wife, against all else. We love and trust God, and we believe His Word—Genesis 2:24. We also don't involve lots of people in our business or talk to them about disagreements or other issues. We do have one or two people each whom we can confide in and share that kind of information with, but that's where it ends. These are also the same people who feel comfortable confiding in us, and when you discover who those people are, it gives you a great sense of comfort. But outside of them, Will and I discuss everything privately, and if something is bothering one of us, we don't walk around for days and weeks pretending that all is well. We talk about everything right away, and this is one of the most important things any married couple can do. Communicate about everything as soon as possible, and find a solution that works for both of you. Consider how your husband feels and try to see things from his point of view, rather than just seeing them from your own. Work hard to find some sort of common ground, and go from there. And remember to communicate, communicate, communicate.

2. Show your husband how much you appreciate him.

Encourage him, lift him up, and always be there when he needs you. When you're making decisions about anything, consider how those decisions will affect him—the same as you would want him to do for you. Do nice things for him— the same as he does for you. Surprise him with a gift or his favorite meal. Will loves, loves, loves fishing, and while I have never been a great cook, Will loves the way I fry catfish (thanks to my mom and grandmother). So when he returns home from a day of fishing, cleans the fish he and his friends have caught, and cuts it up, I rinse off the pieces we're going to have for dinner, season them up, and then deep-fry them. Then I rinse and divide what's left of the uncooked portion into storage bags, and I place them in the freezer. We do this all summer long, at least two days per week, and it gives me joy because it gives *him* joy. I go out of my way to do this and so much more for Will, because he does so many thoughtful things for me. Every now and then, he will also go places that he's not really interested in going, simply because I want to go. And I will sometimes do the same for him, even when I'd much rather be home. But we do this because we try our best to keep each other happy. Once you've been married for a number of years, you tend to inherit many of each other's likes and dislikes anyhow, which means you begin enjoying many of the same things equally. What we shouldn't do, though, is complain about the small stuff. You know, like when your husband lays his clothes around instead of tossing them in the dirty clothes basket? Or wraps his coat or jacket around a kitchen chair instead of hanging it up in the closet? Or when he maybe doesn't clean up behind himself when he cooks? Over the years, I have been guilty of complaining about all three of those things, but I don't comment about any of them as much as I used to, because as I just mentioned, Will does so many thoughtful things for me. He is an amazing husband in so many other ways, too, and he never complains about much of anything. I am certainly not saying he's perfect, and again, neither am I. But he's perfect for me, and we're perfect for each other—and that means everything.

3. Spend quality time together.

As women, we all get busy with our day-to-day responsibilities, but please don't forget about the importance of intimacy. We often hear, too, how important date night is, and I agree with that thinking. This can mean going out for dinner and a movie on the same evening every week, or it can mean getting a sitter for your children and locking yourself away in your bedroom for a few hours—with popcorn, other snacks, and all—watching your favorite romantic comedy or television show. It can even mean getting together for lunch on the same day each week, and I believe married couples should always plan weekend getaways. You can reserve a hotel room in another city or state or enjoy a nice staycation in your own area, either at one of your local hotel establishments—or even at home. You can also take a one-day road trip on Saturday or Sunday, which is another great way to spend time alone. Will and I have done all of the above, but we don't necessarily have one particular day set aside for date night or a date during the day. We tend to go when it's most convenient, but my goal is for us to choose a day that we can stick to and look forward to, no matter what else is going on in our schedules. We do have an annual New Year's Eve tradition, though, and of our twenty-nine years together, we've only spent maybe four or five of them with other people—and that was during our first four to five years of marriage. But for all the other years, we have spent New Year's Eve night at home, with just the two of us. We order wings and a shrimp tray from two different restaurants and pick them up during the early evening hours, and we also buy a veggie tray, dessert, and two bottles of Welch's nonalcoholic sparkling white grape juice. This is always such a special time for us, and we look forward to it every December.

A SCRIPTURE TO HELP YOU

"Love is patient, love is kind. It does not envy, it does not boast, it is not proud. It does not dishonor others, it is not self-seeking, it is not easily angered, it keeps no record of wrongs."

—1 CORINTHIANS 13:4–5 (NIV)

PART THREE

THE
PROFESSIONAL
YOU

CHAPTER 14

Hearing God's Call
and Finding Your Purpose

For a great number of years, I didn't know what my purpose was. Partly because when I was a young girl, I didn't hear much conversation on the subject, and partly because when I became an adult, well…what I mainly focused on was money—how much I could make and how much I would need to live a comfortable life. What I had done was spend my entire childhood deciding on one profession and then quickly changing my mind to another. At one point, I'd been completely sure that I wanted to be an attorney. That is, until I became *very* sure that I wanted to become a doctor. Not just any doctor, either, mind you. No, I wanted to be a gynecologist. A woman's doctor. Something I am not all that surprised about today, given the great passion I have toward helping women.

But my professional brainstorming didn't end there, because after entering junior high school, I decided that what I *really* wanted to be was a TV anchorwoman or a journalist for a newspaper or magazine. Then, in my late teens, I couldn't wait to become a certified public accountant or a paralegal. I wanted to be anything that allowed me to earn an above-average level of income, and I never thought one time about purpose. I never considered the fact that God had placed me here to serve others in a specific way. So I settled my mind on one thing, and one thing only: making as much money as I possibly could.

And I always regretted it.

What's interesting, though, is that of every one of those ten full-time jobs I talked about in Chapter 6, most of them paid about the same salary. One time, I even took a minor pay cut, believing that it would eventually become worth my while in the end. I tried everything I could, but again, it wasn't until I woke up and began thinking a whole lot differently that everything changed for the better. It wasn't until I prayed and thought back to my childhood years, that God began reminding me of what I had enjoyed and what my teachers had told me. I thought long and hard, but it was my sixth grade teacher, Mr. George Groff, whom I thought about most. Because of all my elementary school teachers, it was Mr. Groff who'd always had such positive words to say about my writing. He'd talked about it regularly because if he told us that tonight's writing assignment was half a page, the next morning, I would turn in a whole page. If he told us that the assignment was for a full page, then I would turn in two or three pages. I would do this because I could never seem to write what he was asking for without including lots of detail. My most memorable moment with him, however, was the time he'd given us a writing assignment, and the next day, he asked the entire class to walk our papers up to his desk. But as we returned to our seats, he began thumbing through them, and he came across mine. He skimmed through it and said, "Kim Lawson, why is it when I ask you what time it is, you have to build me an entire clock! Why can't you just say the time and move on?"

My classmates and I laughed, and so did Mr. Groff, but then he went on to say, "I know I give you the business and tease you all the time about your writing, but you really do have a gift for writing and storytelling, and I hope you'll follow through with it." Of course, I never took his words all that seriously, because at eleven years old I didn't believe I was doing anything more than any other student who was trying to get good grades. I didn't think much of it, but when I entered Eisenhower Middle School, I did take journalism as an elective, and I wrote for the school newspaper. I also auditioned for our school's TV anchor position, where I delivered a short news segment each morning for either one school year quarter or an entire semester. I can't remember which, but I do know that I delivered the news right after the bell rang. What I remember, too, is how memorable and enjoyable those times were for me, and that I was so in my element. I am also grateful to my journalism teacher, Mr. Hotlen, for teaching me so much about writing and broadcasting and for encouraging me in such an amazing way. This did prompt me to at least talk about being a writer back then, but my only goals were to write newspaper or magazine articles and possibly deliver broadcast news for a television station. The idea of writing books wasn't something I considered, though.

So, from there, I went on to Auburn High School, entering a gifted program called the Academy, which offered an early-graduating option. I still wasn't sure what I wanted to be as an adult, but because I continued to receive positive feedback about my writing, it did motivate me to check out this whole writing career thing a bit further ... and as you can likely guess, the very first thing I researched was the salary of writers. I wanted to know how much they earned, and when I saw the published average, I thought, "Well, I'm definitely not doing that." I quickly came to this conclusion because I had also researched the salaries of people who majored in business, and what I'd learned was that folks who were graduating with marketing, finance, and business administration degrees were doing pretty well. I knew in my heart what my teachers had told me—almost my entire childhood—but I decided, right then and there, that business would be my major.

But here's something that surprised me: When I finally went back to school to complete my bachelor's degree, I also took an elective course at the University of Wisconsin in Madison called Gender Issues in Management. I took this course alongside the ones I was taking for my degree program with Cardinal Stritch University, so that I could transfer those credits and finish a bit earlier. But God always has a plan and a reason for everything, because, as it turned out, the professor of this course, Professor Margaret Karsten, gave me an A and asked me to send her a letter of permission, allowing her to use my case study as an example for future classes. I was so honored and happy . . . but can you believe that this still didn't help me see that writing was my purpose? To be honest, it had always been my passion, and I just didn't know it, because when I was maybe around nine or ten and in fourth or fifth grade, producers at CBS had announced that they were accepting essay submissions from children for *In the News*, a short news segment for children that aired between cartoons on Saturday mornings. So, I wrote my essay and mailed it off with my little elementary school photo, and not long after, my mom received a call from CBS saying that my essay had been chosen to have an excerpt read from it, and that the segment would air nationally that coming weekend. To this day, I can still remember the globe turning and the theme music playing and then seeing my handwritten essay on notebook paper with my photo lying on top of it. But again, none of these moments helped me see that writing was my purpose.

Which was the reason that even after I finished my Gender Issues in Management course at UW Madison, three more years passed before I sat down to begin writing my first novel, *Behind Closed Doors.* That was in April 1995, and ironically, this was only one month before I turned thirty years old, so I had spent all my twenties ignoring the many hints, nudges, and outright confirmation that God had been giving me for years. He'd placed all the right people in my path, all of whom had encouraged me and offered me great writing opportunities, but I hadn't paid much attention to any of them. Because unlike for many writers I know, writing wasn't a lifelong dream of mine, so instead of hearing God's call, I did what I wanted. Or maybe I actually had heard His call and had simply ignored it, because I believed wholeheartedly that if I tried to become a writer, I'd barely be able to pay my rent.

But thankfully, God never gave up on me, and once I did begin listening to what He had so profoundly placed in my heart, I couldn't think about much else. The idea of writing became my priority, and I could hardly wait to get started. I soon became so passionate about my purpose that when I finally sat down to begin writing the first chapter of my book, I wrote every single weeknight, every weekend, and on holidays. I did this while still working full-time, for seven whole months until my manuscript was complete. After that, I began searching for a literary agent, because what I had learned through my research was that editors at major publishing houses don't prefer to read unsolicited manuscripts. At the time, most publishers received hundreds of manuscripts per week, so they wanted you to have agency representation. That way, they could be sure that your work had gone through somewhat of a vetting process.

So I did my homework, seeking out literary agents who were already representing female authors who wrote commercial fiction, and I compiled a list of fourteen of them to submit my manuscript to. I wrote the requested query letters, and in some cases I included a chapter or two. I packaged everything up, mailed them, and waited. But then something dawned on me. I thought, *Surely all fourteen of them will want to represent me, so how am I going to decide on one of them and turn down the other thirteen?*

Even today, at this very moment, it's hard to believe how naïve I was about the whole process. But this had truly been my thinking ... until that first rejection letter arrived in our mailbox.

And then another.

And yet another after that.

Those dismal letters kept coming, and soon I'd been rejected by all fourteen agents that I had queried.

All fourteen.

So at that point, I took a step back and reluctantly accepted my rude awakening. But I was deeply disappointed, because I then knew how hard getting published was going to be. Still, I continued to move forward. I knew that editors didn't want to receive manuscripts directly, but since I couldn't find a literary agent, I didn't see where I had anything to lose. The worst that could happen was that they would reject me, too, so I compiled a new listing. I sought out editors who had acquired books in the contemporary women's fiction genre and mailed each package.

And once again, I waited.

And then, I received rejection letter, after rejection letter, after rejection letter, until I had been rejected by all of them. Most were form letters, but there was one that I will never forget, which said, "You've got a lot of talent for writing and rendering interesting characters and storylines." But then the editor went on to say that her plate was full with debut fiction.

Now, I do know that this was still a no, but nonetheless, this editor's response made me feel somewhat better than the other rejection letters had. Her words gave me a small ray of hope, even if only for a few minutes. Because, unfortunately, it wasn't long before that little bit of hope had vanished. It was gone, and not only was I disappointed, I was completely discouraged. As far as I was concerned, I had done all I could do, and it was time to move on. Which was a sad moment for me, because I had so enjoyed writing my book, and I was looking forward to writing another.

I even debated whether I should try querying more agents or whether I should give up, and eventually I chose the latter. I decided that all of this had been a nice idea, but it was also time for me to figure out what I was going to do next. It is true that, by then, I knew that writing was a big part of who I was and that it was a huge part of my purpose, but I also didn't believe anyone would ever want to publish my work. So, I began applying to MBA programs. I decided to work toward a degree that would take me farther away from my purpose than I already was. I realize now how unwise that was, but my thinking was, if I couldn't get my book published, a master's degree would help me move farther along in city government where I worked or at another place of employment.

But thank God for my mom and Will, because when my mom heard me saying that I was done with the whole writing thing and realized how serious I was, she said, "I don't know anything about publishing, but what I do know is that we have been passing around copies of your manuscript to women here locally, and so many of them have said that they couldn't put it down until they finished it. So that has to mean something, and I just don't think you should give up."

Those were the wonderful words she told me, but after all that I have shared with you about my mom thus far, I'm sure I don't have to tell you that this is the same woman who had me thinking, as a toddler, that I could move mountains. My mom constantly encouraged me, my entire life, telling me that I could do anything. So if my book was awful, was she really going to tell me that? I didn't think so, which was the reason that, even though I listened, I had no plans to continue trying to get published. I was done. But then once Will discovered that I was really giving up, he said, "Why can't you take your business background, start your own company, and publish the book yourself?"

To this day, I'm not sure what prompted Will to say this, because it wasn't something I had thought much about doing. To be honest, I had never entertained the idea of self-publishing because I knew that, in order to self-publish the correct way, a large investment would be needed. If we were to publish a book that would look as professional as those being published by the New York industry, it was going to cost us. But Will didn't see the problem. To him, it was well worth it, so I purchased every book I could find on self-publishing and read them cover to cover. Ultimately, though, it was *The Self-Publishing Manual* by Dan

Poynter that taught me everything on the subject. After that, I did more research, trying to figure out how we would get my book out on a national level, versus just distributing it locally or regionally. Especially since Will had decided to borrow money from his 401(k) account, we were taking out a small loan from our credit union, and we were going to have to use some of our personal savings. But even once I realized that self-publishing was possible, fear started to consume me. I wanted to publish my book, but I also worried that no one would buy it.

So I finally asked Will a question. "What if this doesn't work? Have you thought about that?"

And his response was, "If it doesn't work, then you'll just move on to something else. But do you want to go, say, ten years down the road still wondering if you could have been successful with this?"

I thought about everything Will was saying, as well as what my mom had told me, and from there, my decision was made. I founded my publishing business in June 1996, only six months after I had finished writing the book. I was still working full-time as a financial analyst for the City of Rockford's community development department, so I worked all day there and then worked all evening on my self-publishing process. Sometimes I worked until well after midnight, but I loved every minute of it. I was excited, and by August, I was ready to submit my final book cover design and the typeset book pages to the printer I had selected. We had also booked a banquet hall for October 27 for my opening reception and sent out hundreds of invitations to all the people we knew. It didn't hurt that I worked for the city, because our mayor at the time, the honorable Mayor Charles Box, and one of our state assemblymen, Doug Scott, who had

once worked as the city's legal director, had both agreed to
attend, which meant that I was able to include their names in
the press release I sent out to our local media. I wasn't sure what
to expect, but soon, I received responses from our newspaper
and our local ABC, NBC, and CBS affiliates, which at the time,
were WREX, WTVO, and WIFR, respectively. The *Rockford
Register Star* interviewed me and printed a full-page article,
and all three television affiliates came to the book reception. It
was all a dream come true, and I mean, talk about God ordering
my steps. Because had I stayed with the company that hadn't
treated me so well (the one I spoke about in Chapter 6), I might
not have learned about the job with the city at all.

But because of the publicity I was blessed to have (thanks to
the wonderful Mayor Box and Assemblyman Scott), more than
five hundred people came out to support my reception. We were
hoping for great attendance, but when it happened, I was still
pleasantly surprised about it. And if that hadn't been enough,
once Will and I were home that Sunday evening, and we had
watched coverage of the reception on each of the news channels,
he told me about another big bright idea he had.

"So, you know when you go to work on Tuesday, you're going
to have to give your two weeks' notice, right?"

We'd both taken off the next day as a vacation day—that
Monday—so this was the reason he'd specifically mentioned
"Tuesday." But all I could do was stare at him and think, *Wow,
he's really, really lost it this time*, because did he really think I
was going to quit my job? Did he think I was going to walk away
from it, all while knowing that I could still fail as an author?

I just didn't get it, and although I so very much appreciated
Will and the fact that he believed in me and my book—more

than I did—I couldn't imagine us becoming a one-income household. But Will never wavered in his thinking and said matter-of-factly, "If you don't give this one hundred percent of your time, I don't think you'll be successful with it. And no, we won't have the same amount of money we're used to having, but we'll still be able to pay our bills, and we'll be fine."

He told me how he felt and then left the decision up to me. So the next day I discussed it with my mom and also with a couple of friends, but I was still afraid to take such a big risk. My faith wasn't nearly where it needed to be, so instead of considering how well things might work out, I thought about the many things that could go wrong.

But on that Tuesday morning, October 29, 1996, I went to work and submitted my resignation. I stepped out on faith...and I have been writing full-time ever since. I then went on to sell that first printing of three thousand copies fairly quickly to many of the amazing, independent black-owned bookstores that were still open. Emma Rodgers, who owned Black Images in Dallas, Texas—whom I will always be grateful to—became my biggest bookstore supporter, and she immediately began recommending my book to her colleagues who owned bookstores in Texas and in other cities around the country. The larger retail chains, libraries, and wholesalers began ordering it, too, and by the first quarter of 1997, I had signed with a literary agent who sold my second book, *Here and Now*, to an editor with Kensington Publishing. And while this editor ended up leaving the company before I submitted my completed manuscript, Karen Thomas had been hired, and she immediately became a blessing to me in more ways than one. Then, as God would have it, we found ourselves working together again in 2009 when she acquired four of my books for Hachette Book Group, and I am so happy to have her editing *The Woman God Created You to Be* as well. However, shortly after my agent sold my second novel, she then sold *Behind Closed Doors* to the amazing Paul Coates, founder of Black Classic Press in Baltimore, Maryland. But before I stopped printing my self-published edition, it had sold ten thousand copies within the first six months of being on sale.

So in the end, everything turned out better than I expected, and as you know, the book you're reading now is my twenty-eighth title. But imagine how differently things could have evolved had I continued following my *own* plans. Have you maybe experienced something like this, too? Are you focused on what you believe is best for you versus what *God* wants for you? If so, let me say this:

Our plans will never compare to what God has planned for us. Never.

Why? Because He knows what He wants and needs from us, and this is the reason I love Proverbs 19:21 (NLT), which says, "You can make many plans, but the LORD'S purpose will prevail."

So all we have to do is hear His call and wait for His instructions. And do you remember those gifts, talents, and abilities I spoke about in the Introduction to this book? Well, God wants us to use those gifts, talents, and abilities to serve others.

"God has given each of you a gift from his great variety of spiritual gifts. Use them well to serve one another."
—1 PETER 4:10 (NLT)

He wants us to use everything He has given us, so that we can help as many people as possible.

He wants us to trust *Him*.

And do what He has placed us on this beautiful earth to do.

THREE THINGS YOU CAN DO

1. Discover your purpose.

Even when I was a child, I loved conversing with others and asking questions about things I wasn't familiar with, and in school, I was always getting into trouble for talking way too much in class. But now, churches, libraries, colleges and universities, and various women's organizations invite me to serve as their keynote speaker at many different events. Not to mention, right after my mom and I left my first formal speaking engagement, which occurred not long after my first book was released, she said these words to me: "Whenever you're going to speak, I want to be there." This, of course, inspired me because I knew my mom believed that I had a gift for speaking. But to be honest, the only reason I had accepted that first speaking invitation was because I'd read somewhere that speaking tended to help authors promote their work. Since I had said yes, though, and my mom had gone with me, she was able to share her feelings about my speaking ability, which gave me more confidence toward accepting future invitations. So please know that hearing what others think of your gifts and talents can make a great difference for you. And equally important is the fact that so much of what you loved doing as a child has everything to do with your assigned purpose. Think back to those early years of your life and pray for God to show you what He wants you to do. Think about what you loved. Was it cleaning? If so, are you preparing to start your cleaning service? Was it cooking? If so, have you started your catering business? Was it singing? Or painting? Or maybe you had a great love for numbers? If so, have you considered going back to school to become an accountant? Do you maybe love planning parties? If so, do you own an event planning business? Or maybe you always loved sewing. If so, are you designing your own clothing? There's something else you should remember, too. God can use anyone or anything to push you into your purpose: that company that laid you off, that friend who betrayed you, or even the very messy divorce you may have just gone through. God will use whatever He sees fit to elevate and empower you, so that He can carry you completely into your destiny.

2. Don't let money be your decision maker.

When I was younger, I sometimes quoted the first part of 1 Timothy 6:10 incorrectly. I would say, "Money is the root of all evil," but the correct words are "For the love of money is the root of all evil" (KJV). I once even made the mistake of misquoting this verse on a national TV talk show. It wasn't until I watched the recorded episode that I finally realized my error, and I haven't misstated that scripture since. But the reason I wanted to point this out is because there is definitely a difference. Having money and being obsessed with money are not the same thing. Because if you're earning money in an honest way, and you're using it to take care of yourself and to help those in need, then to me, there is nothing wrong with working hard and making enough money to also buy some of the things you want. But when it comes to choosing a certain career or doing a certain job primarily because it will pay us a large sum of money, well, this shouldn't be our only motive. Instead, our choices should have everything to do with the purpose God has given us. So please don't do what I once did. Don't let money be the deciding factor when you are trying to discover your calling.

3. Never forget that you were placed on this earth to serve others.

For many years, Will and I have tried to help as many people as we can, because we believe that when God blesses you through your purpose, He wants you to be a blessing to someone else. This does not mean feeling obligated to help people who choose not to be good stewards of their money (buying things they don't need or taking expensive vacations and then not paying their rent, mortgage, or utilities), and it also doesn't mean that we should allow ourselves to be used or taken advantage of simply because we are someone's family member or friend. But when we know for sure that someone is less fortunate—that they've lost their job or become ill, for example—we should help them. We should do this whether they ask for our assistance or not, because at some point in time, any of us could find ourselves in need. We should also contribute to our churches and other nonprofit organizations. Will and I tithe at our church, and we donate to various charities. I want to mention, too, though, that your purpose and level of service doesn't always have to revolve around finances, and it doesn't always mean being out in the forefront. Sometimes it may involve serving ten or twenty people versus ten or twenty million. Sometimes service can mean becoming the key person in the background, and there is nothing wrong with that. Or serving others might simply mean taking an elderly person to a doctor's appointment, cooking food and delivering it to the sick and shut-in, volunteering to help single mothers who might be struggling in one area or another, or donating clothes to a homeless shelter. God can call us to do anything at all, and our job is to be ready and willing to answer Him.

A SCRIPTURE TO HELP YOU

"And we know that all things work together for good to those who love God, to those who are the called according to *His* purpose."

—ROMANS 8:28 (NKJV)

CHAPTER 15

Fear, Faith, and Trusting God, No Matter What

In the last chapter, I talked about being afraid to self-publish, but what that really meant was that I was afraid to step out on faith. It meant that my longtime faith in God only went so far, and that I only trusted Him when I knew I was making safe decisions. When I wasn't taking any risks, and the chance of failing was very slim. My faith was lukewarm at best, and this is the reason that many of us struggle as much as we do. It is the reason that so, so many of us haven't started women's ministries, written books, recorded songs, founded businesses, applied for job promotions, or gone back to school to further our education. We haven't done any of the above, because, well...

We're scared to death.

We're frightened out of our minds, because we believe that if we do any of what we want to do, we will fail miserably. We are afraid to leave our comfort zones, which means that we are telling God, loudly and clearly, that we don't trust Him to do what He says He will do. We don't believe that He has adequately equipped us to handle the purpose He has given us. We don't believe that He truly does give us the desires of our hearts—those that fall within His eternal will. No, what we do is walk around inside our little self-made circles, making sure we don't step anywhere outside of them. We become both a prisoner and the warden. We live in fear, and we believe that being average is all we can ever expect. We decide that we just don't have what it takes to accomplish anything more than that.

But, my dear sister, I want you to know something: Fear is not of God. Fear is simply a sly trick of the enemy. It's what he uses to stop you from doing God's work. He tells you what you can't do, why you can't do it, and that if you attempt to do it anyway, you'll be making the biggest mistake of your life. He will even send naysayers your way. You know, those people who don't mind telling you every reason in the world why your vision or idea won't work?

The enemy will also use the spirit of procrastination to stifle you even further. Because what I've learned is that once we begin procrastinating, it gives the enemy a lot more time to make his case. It gives him ample opportunity to place more doubt in our minds and more belittling thoughts in our spirits, driving a whole new level of fear deep inside our souls. By procrastinating, we allow the enemy to take over our lives, and we totally disregard what God has already told us and confirmed in our hearts.

I know this to be true, because once I'd made the decision to self-publish my first book, my faith and confidence were in a good place. I was moving along just fine, and all was going well. But then, about a month before our opening reception, the first printing of three thousand books arrived at our home, and the enemy showed up again. He didn't do it right away, though, because the day before, when I had received a call from the trucking company letting me know that I needed to have a lot of people ready to help remove the boxes from the semitruck, I couldn't have been more excited. For twenty-four hours, I hadn't been able to think about much else, and once Will arrived home from work and my mom and two brothers came to our house straight from their jobs, the truck arrived, and we carried box after box inside our home and into our guest bedroom. Of course, though, as I write this, I am smiling because of how supportive Junior and Mike have always been. They are my dear brothers, but I love them the way a mother loves her children, and even now, some of the most heartwarming, hilarious, and best conversations I have are with the two of them.

But as far as the books we carried into our home, well, they were everywhere! Still, I was excited and so were Will, my mom, and my brothers. It was a happy day, and maybe a week or so earlier, my mom had told me that she wanted me to sign the first book I pulled out of the box for her. I knew she was proud of what I had accomplished, yet I remember thinking how strange her request had seemed, because she never asked for anything. I certainly would have given her everything imaginable if I could, but again, her request wasn't normal, at least not for her.

Little did I know, though, my first book would be the only book she would be able to fully celebrate with me, and it was the only book she was able to read without a struggle, because by the time I'd finished writing my second book, her brain tumor had already begun affecting her vision. *Behind Closed Doors* was also the only book she was able to help me with, as she would come by after work to label boxes and package up some of the books that needed to be shipped to bookstores, distributors, and wholesalers.

I know I'm supposed to be talking about fear and telling you about my own personal experiences, but I just need to delay that story for a minute to say this: God always knows what He is doing. He knew that by the time my second book would be released, we would have just learned that my mom's doctors had done all they could do for her, and that unless God decided otherwise, she wasn't going to get better. So, He allowed her to enjoy everything relating to my very first book—my writing process, the self-publishing process, our opening reception, and even the loading up of all three of our cars—hers, Will's, and mine—so that we could transport boxes of ordered books out to UPS. God allowed her to witness and experience so much of what she had, in fact, hoped and prayed for me, and I am eternally grateful to Him for that.

So, as planned, I signed that first book for my mom, and then I signed copies for Will and my brothers. (This is still something I laugh about, though, because remember how my mom had always said, "Will comes even before me?" She was definitely sincere about that, but when those books arrived, she thought about *herself* for a change. And we're so happy she did.)

Not long after I signed all four books, though, my mom, Junior, and Mike went home, and a few hours later, Will went to bed. But I was feeling like a kid at Christmastime. I was also still excited and somewhat shocked that I had actually published a book. So I couldn't help walking down our hallway to our guest bedroom, just so I could take one more look. But when I turned on the light, things appeared a lot differently than they had earlier. Books seemed to be stacked all over the place, and all I could think was *I must have been completely out of my mind.* Because who in the world was going to buy all of these books? I began to worry much more than I had, and soon I became irritated with Will, wondering why I had allowed him to talk me into doing something so ridiculous. I became more and more fearful by the second. But as I stood there, I thought about my mom and grandmother and what both of them would tell me when I thought I was facing something way too difficult. They would say, "Honey, sometimes you have to double your determination, and keep right on going."

So that's exactly what I did. I turned out the light, walked back down the hallway—and doubled my determination. The books were printed and paid for, the invitations were about to be mailed out for the reception, and there was no turning back. And for the most part, that way of thinking, along with my strong faith in God, is what has kept me writing books every year since. That is, until, Wednesday, October 5, 2016, at 4:15 a.m. That was the moment I heard the words "Hearing God's Call, and Finding Your Purpose," and glanced over at the clock on my nightstand. The words were so real and clear that I couldn't ignore them. So I reached over and turned on my light and then got up to grab some paper and something to write with. My handbag was sitting on the chair in our bedroom, so I rummaged through it until I located a pen and a banking envelope. It was all I could find, but at that point, I just wanted to write down the words that God had given me before I forgot them. Especially since, after all the years that I had been writing, this was the first time He had awakened me from my sleep with specific words. This was also the first time I knew for *sure* that He wanted me to write my first nonfiction book. I'd had brief thoughts about writing nonfiction in the past, which was the reason I had begun asking my attorney to include language in all my publishing contracts, so that if I ever wanted to publish that genre on my own, I could. I had no idea what I would write about, though, because to be honest, I still had no real desire to write nonfiction. Not to mention, since I was already signed with a publisher, I knew I could submit my work to them, the same as I was doing with my other books. I could also submit it to most other publishing houses in the industry. But there was something inside me that told me otherwise. Then, nearly two years later, while Will and I were traveling on the book tour for the final title in my Reverend Curtis Black series, I prayed for direction. We were on a plane, and I closed my eyes, asking God if I should submit this book to my publisher or if I should self-publish it, and I instantly heard, "You are going to self-publish it, because this will be another part of your testimony."

When I heard those words, they sort of startled me, and I instantly opened my eyes. I could hear them the same as when I heard my own thoughts, but these words entered my mind too quickly to have come from me. It may sound strange to some, but it wasn't as though I was brainstorming or going back and forth about what I should do. The words simply entered my mind— only a split second after I asked God my question. I heard them very distinctly, and I also knew He would give me everything I needed during this process. I knew this because, for years, I have been published by three major publishing houses, so why would I even consider self-publishing any of my books unless God had placed it in my heart to do so? Yes, I had self-published my first title because I hadn't seen any other alternative, but why would I write the last book of my current contract and not submit my next book proposal or outline to my publisher the way I have been doing for years? Or submit it to a faith-based publishing house, even?

I will say, though, that these questions did make me a bit uneasy. Not because I didn't know how to self-publish, but because I knew it was going to add a lot more work to my plate. Still, no matter how much I tried to weigh my options and follow my *own* plans, God's instructions remained intact. They wouldn't go away, and as you'll remember, when He gave me the assignment of writing this book, that wouldn't go away, either. Yet, as I prepared to work on my first nonfiction title, I became more afraid, and I procrastinated. As I look back, though, I now realize just how good it was for me to take an entire year off from writing. I needed a break, and because I took one, I feel more energized and passionate about writing than I have in a very long time. So, in this case, procrastination was a good thing.

Still, once I did begin writing again, I struggled with lots of fear, both about writing in a genre that I had never written in before and about the idea of self-publishing in a new era. I allowed fear to invade my thinking, and there were times when I became so afraid that I thought twice about doing any of it. But then I began outlining the chapters and writing them, and I enjoyed the process so much that I looked forward to it.

Every single day.

I still experienced some moments of fear, but I also remembered that fear is merely a four-letter word and nothing more. Yes, I do know that fear will cripple us—if we let it. And that it is also a natural feeling for all human beings. But when God has called us to do something, we must trust Him and do it afraid. We must trust Him from the bottoms of our souls and have faith in Him at all times.

We must believe God and not the enemy.

THREE THINGS YOU CAN DO

1. Don't let fear consume you.

I can't count the number of times that I have allowed fear to consume me, which is the reason I am encouraging you to never do this. Yes, fear is a natural emotion, but if we make up our minds to not be overtaken by it, we will be so much better off. If we refuse to walk in fear, we will hear God, follow His lead, and accomplish more than we could ever imagine. If we refuse to allow the enemy to have his way with us, saturating our minds with worry, dread, and anxiety, we will find the courage to do every bit of what God has asked us to do. If you become God-fearing—genuinely and wholeheartedly—you won't have to fear anything else. Or even if you do become fearful (because we all experience weak moments), fear won't stop you completely. It won't prevent you from achieving what God wants you to achieve or hinder any of the wonderful success He has planned for you.

2. Keep your faith strong and consistent.

Doing this every single day will sustain you in ways that wouldn't be possible otherwise. Because if we sincerely exercise our faith, we will find ourselves empowered and able to do our most difficult tasks. We will have courage to fight what appear to be losing battles and we will know, without question, that we can accomplish every aspect of what God has called us to do, regardless of our expertise or lack thereof. Because if God calls us to do something, He will give us *all* the skills and qualifications we need to get things done. We must also remember James 2:26 (NKJV), because just as the scripture says, "Faith without works is dead." So, even though we may have total faith in God and strong faith in what we are trying to accomplish, we still have to do our part. We still have to make a commitment, remain dedicated, and work hard—doing all that is required.

3. Hear God and trust Him completely.

So, nearly two decades ago, two of my books went to auction, and for those who may not be familiar with this process, let me explain. What it means is that more than one publishing house was interested in acquiring my work, so Elaine Koster, my amazing literary agent, scheduled meetings with all of them. I flew to New York, and over a three-day period, she and I met with nine different editors and publishing groups. Then, even though I knew in my heart of hearts which editor was truly passionate about my writing and who I felt the best about in my spirit, I went against what God was telling me. Eight of those publishing imprints placed a bid in the auction, and I chose the one that was offering me four times what my former publisher had offered me per book. The editor and publisher that I loved and with whom I felt the most comfortable were offering about three times the offer I had received from my former publisher, but again, I chose the more lucrative deal. And I soon regretted it. I did what I've already asked you not to do: I went with the money. I allowed *money* to be my deciding factor, and about a year later, things turned disastrous, and I ended up leaving the company. But thankfully, we serve a God who is full of grace and mercy, as He worked out everything. I wasn't sure what to expect, but when my agent went back to that wonderful editor at HarperCollins Publishers whom I had passed on, she basically told Elaine that their offer was still on the table. Then, as it turned out, not only did I sign with Harper, they ended up publishing eleven of my books, and I was blessed to spend eight incredible years with them. So please, when you hear God, trust His judgment and act accordingly. Trust Him with every part of your being.

A SCRIPTURE TO HELP YOU

"This is my command—be strong and courageous! Do not be afraid or discouraged. For the Lord your God is with you wherever you go."

—JOSHUA 1:9 (NLT)

CHAPTER 16

Pray, Plan, Practice—Proceed

What I've discovered over the years is that whether you know your purpose or not, there are certain steps you should take to accomplish your goals. If you don't know your purpose, then, of course, praying is what you need to continue doing until you discover it. But if you do know your purpose, and you're ready to begin fulfilling it, then you'll want to do the following:

Pray, plan, practice, and proceed.

This is what I call my 4-P Process, and I must say, it has made a world of difference for me. It helps me stay focused and organized, which is very important, because without structure, we can sometimes become frustrated and confused about what to do first or next. We can also become a Jill of all trades and mistress of none. Yes, I realize that God has, in fact, given each of us the many gifts, talents, and abilities that I have been speaking about all along, but I don't believe He wants us to do everything. What I believe is that when we make up our minds to follow our purpose, and we realize how much work it will require, we sometimes begin looking at other options. We look for something safer and easier. We search for things that we know we can do quickly and those that won't require much effort.

I know I've done this in the past myself, because let's face it, many of us want to finish what we're doing as quickly as possible, so that we can begin reaping great rewards—as quickly as we possibly can. We want to enjoy life and not spend any more time laboring, performing, or producing than we have to. But what I also know is that anything worth having requires a huge amount of hard work. And in order to offer God and everyone else the very best of who we are, we must operate in excellence and not in mediocrity, which means we must do our fair share of praying, planning, and practicing before we even consider proceeding with anything.

This is the reason that just before I begin writing each day, I take my Bible into my prayer closet, I read a passage of scripture, and then I pray. I'm also very specific, so for example, when I write fiction, I recite the Lord's Prayer, and then I ask God to give me the words He wants me to say and the scenes He wants me to write, so that they can help as many people as possible. I ask Him to allow whichever book I'm working on to be my best-written book yet. And when I say best written, I'm not just referring to craft and technique. What I'm also doing is asking God to give me the ability to write the kind of message that He wants my readers to receive and be blessed by in one way or another. This has always been my hope and prayer, even when writing about some of the controversial topics and characters I have centered some of my stories on.

Then, for this book, my prayer became more detailed. I have continued to begin each day by reciting the Lord's Prayer, but I also ask God to give me the words He wants me to say and the wisdom I need to articulate them—specifically in the way that He wants them to be written. I ask Him to give me the kind of

words that will inspire, motivate, and encourage women everywhere. I then ask Him to pour those words into my mind, heart,
soul, and spirit and to allow them to flow through my fingers,
into my keyboard, onto my screen, and then onto the printed
page. I realize that this may sound like a lot to some, but what I
can tell you for sure is that staying prayerful every single day, in
this manner, is the only reason I was able to write *The Woman
God Created You to Be* in the way I believe it was destined to
be written.

I do this during the actual chapter-writing process, and I
also pray this way when I'm preparing to write the initial outline of a book. So, for me, praying is step 1, creating my two-
to three-page synopsis is step 2, and outlining is step 3 of my
4-P Process—what I call the praying, planning, and practicing
stages. Actually, my outlining process sort of becomes both my
planning and practicing stages, as this is when I begin creating
the overall synopsis for each individual chapter. I don't outline
all of them, but I do summarize about one-half. So, for example,
if I believe my book will average about thirty chapters, I will outline fifteen. If I know it will average forty, I will outline twenty.
Then, once I begin step 4, the proceeding stage—writing the
actual chapters—I feel a lot more equipped to do so because
of the praying, planning, and practicing I've already done. Yes,
there are times when I am led to write something other than
what I've included in my outline, but having a detailed summary
still helps me tremendously. Then, once I've written all of my
outlined chapters (the first fifteen or twenty), I will outline three
to five more chapters at a time and write them. After that, I will
outline three to five more, and so on, until I have written the
entire book. Although, what I need to make clear is that, once

I've written the last word of the last chapter, this becomes my first draft; which is the reason that the initial writing of the book sort of feels as though I am in both the practicing and proceeding stages. I say this because once I finish writing my first draft, this is when so much of the real work begins. This is when I read through the entire manuscript, marking up every page—and sometimes every single line on a page—with a red pen. This is when I incorporate major rewrites and other revisions, prior to submitting the final manuscript to my content editor.

But I don't just pray, plan, practice and proceed with writing, I do this for everything. When I am asked to serve as keynote speaker for events, I pray for God to give me the words that He wants me to share with a specific audience, I begin outlining my speech, and I practice it, over and over again, right up until the day of my speaking engagement. We should also pray, plan, practice, and proceed when God leads us to start a ministry or a business. We should pray, research anything that we aren't familiar with, study, and then begin writing a ministry or business plan. We should also write a marketing plan, because even when God assigns us the task of heading up a ministry, we need to prepare ourselves the same as we would in the business world. We need to figure out how we will reach the people He wants us to serve, letting them know that our particular kind of help is available.

Then, once we have our plans in place, we should begin practicing, rehearsing, and doing the same thing, over and over. Because you know that old saying, right? "Practice makes perfect." Yes, we've already established in an earlier chapter that none of us will ever be perfect, but practicing helps us become the best we *can* be. It helps us become great women in ministry and great businesswomen, and it also makes us more capable of serving others.

By praying, planning, and practicing, we will also have much less chance of becoming overwhelmed, disorganized, and confused about what it is we need to do. We should pray and remember 1 Corinthians 14:33 (NKJV), which says, "For God is not *the author* of confusion but of peace, as in all the churches of the saints."

We should also remember what Proverbs 16:9 (NLT) says about the steps we take. "We can make our plans, but the LORD determines our steps." This is so very true, and it is the reason that *praying* is the first step of my 4-P Process. Because when we pray for direction, God will tell us what our remaining steps should be. He will show us exactly what He has designed for us to do—and how to do it—and we won't have to deal with a huge amount of trial and error. We will certainly make a few mistakes here and there, but we won't make nearly as many as we would on our own. If we pray and do our part (plan and practice) before proceeding with anything, God will steer us in the right direction every single time.

He will guide us every step of the way until the very end.

THREE THINGS YOU CAN DO

1. When you pray, be specific.

By now, you know how much I believe in this particular way of praying, but because "pray" is the first step of my 4-P Process, I wanted to elaborate a bit further. When I knew I wanted God to bring a certain kind of man into my life, I didn't pray for just any man, I prayed for God to bring me a

man who would love me as much as I loved him. And now, in
my daily prayers, when I am asking God to heal others from
illnesses, I include the words "spiritually, mentally, emotionally, and physically." And the same applies for my purpose and professional life, which is the reason that when I
pray about my writing or speaking assignments, my prayers
are just as detailed. They are specific because I am trusting
God to bless me with a specific outcome. So, for example, if
you know your purpose in life is to start a women's ministry,
then you could ask God to tell you what kind of women's
ministry (one that will help single women, married women,
divorced women, mothers, etc.). After that you could ask
Him to show you how He wants you to reach out to women
and where He wants you to hold your first meeting. You
could then ask Him what topic He wants you to discuss first
and then pray that He will grow your ministry in a way that
will allow you to help hundreds or even thousands of women.
You could pray that your ministry will forever be about Him
and His will. And please always remember that your job,
career, or hobby can also be your ministry, because God can
use anything or anybody to help you serve others.

2. Learn everything you can.

This is imperative, because whenever you are called by God
to do anything or even if we're simply referring to the job or
career you have now, you should learn every single thing
you can about what it is you are preparing to do. This is why
when I wrote my first book and ultimately self-published it,
I spent about seven hundred dollars on reference books. I

did this in only a matter of months, and I read many of them cover to cover. I studied and researched everything I could about starting a business, self-publishing, and book marketing, and I believe that placed me in a much better position to succeed. Even now, when I am embarking on a new project that I haven't done before, I Google lots and lots of articles and blog posts, reading one after another. I make it a point to learn from every angle. I study people who are already doing what I'm aspiring or planning to do, and I research what has worked for them and what hasn't. I spend days and weeks finding answers to all my questions, and then I do more research. So, for example, if you want to start a catering business, Google everything you can on the subject. If you want to start a ministry for women in recovery for drug and alcohol addiction, you can Google "How to start a ministry for women in recovery for drug and alcohol addiction." If you want to write a novel, Google "How to write a novel," or "How to write a book." If you want to open a day care center, Google that particular information. If you want to study the best ways to ask for a promotion from your employer, you can Google that as well. If you want to continue your education, Google the type of training or degree you want to pursue, and then begin researching and comparing the costs and curriculums of all the schools you have an interest in. Research, study, and research again— for everything. Also, do hire experts for anything that falls outside of your own set of gifts, talents, and abilities, so that you can execute every aspect of your business or ministry in a professional manner.

3. Write it, organize it, and execute it.

Habakkuk 2:2 talks about writing the vision and making it plain, and during your planning stage, I highly recommend doing this. I am encouraging you to pray, listen for God's instructions, and then write down everything He reveals to you. I do this for my outlines, speeches, business and marketing plans, and budgets. Writing things down will also help you stay organized, and it will allow you to see what you possibly need to add, delete, or rearrange. What I've discovered, too, is that writing down my vision on paper makes it feel that much more real. So before I begin writing a new book, I head to the office store to purchase a brand-new spiral notebook. Nothing fancy, just a college-ruled 9½×6 version that has five sections. I begin my early synopsis process, and sometimes I do a bit of outlining, too, before I actually type it in a Word document. I do the same thing for my speeches, and for other projects I am embarking on. Then, for the last couple of Decembers, I've gone to the office store to purchase more formal planners so that I can begin strategizing the first part of the coming year. Because for me, writing out my plan and organizing it makes it a lot easier to execute. It helps me see my overall vision a whole lot better.

A SCRIPTURE TO HELP YOU

"Commit to the LORD whatever you do, and he will establish your plans."

—PROVERBS 16:3 (NIV)

CHAPTER 17

Your Brand and Your Reputation

I have always believed that, as women, we have an obligation to uphold and protect our reputations. As girls, we were taught to have respect for ourselves so that others would respect us in return, and to me, that same thinking should apply in adulthood. We should also show great respect for everyone around us and safeguard the brands and platforms God has given us.

But sadly, this doesn't always happen—online or in person. So I'm just going to state what most of us already know: When it comes to creating a social media presence for ourselves and our businesses, there is a right way and a wrong way to do it.

There is a right way and a wrong way to *present* your brand and platform.

I say this because regardless of whether our purpose requires us to offer products or services, we should use certain protocol. We should exhibit the highest level of professionalism and present ourselves to the masses as true women of God.

We should keep things classy.

And ethical.

At all times.

Otherwise, people can and will choose not to work with us.

And rightfully so.

Remember how in Chapter 1 I talked about having a true relationship with God and not just on Sunday? Well, this applies to social media, too. What it means is that we need to be careful in terms of what we post to our friends and followers. I sometimes see a huge number of alarming comments, and I know you've seen them, too. Professional women posting negative jabs at clients whom they're having a disagreement with—without naming them, of course. Professional women cursing on their social media posts, sometimes only minutes after posting a scripture or professing their awesome love for God. I also see professional women posting inappropriate or insulting photos and memes, and then when they learn that someone is offended by them, they upload another post letting folks know that if they don't like what they see or read on *their* page, they can simply unfollow them ... because they can *do* and *say* whatever they want on their page.

This is very true, but what I know, too, is that many women are like me: They will, in fact, unfollow women who show themselves to be combative or hostile. Or if they don't unfollow or block them, they will scroll past all controversial or confrontational social media posts, never clicking "like" or commenting on any of them.

And here's another really popular thing I see: Professional women posting sarcastic, not-so-nice comments to their unspecified clients, family members, or friends—people they want to blast publicly without saying the person's name.

In today's age, we see it all, and while we are all adults and we can, of course, do whatever we choose, what I can tell you is this: When I see women doing any of the above, I immediately shy away from them. Some are truly talented, even. Many are so gifted that I would love to hire them for all kinds of freelance work and other projects. But I don't, because I'm too afraid that I'll soon find myself facing some sort of harsh confrontation, or worse, I'll wake up one morning only to learn that the person I hired has posted nasty comments online about me or our business relationship. I also see women on social media who offer great services whom I would love to recommend to colleagues of mine, but again, I'm too afraid to recommend them because I don't want to make an introduction that might end badly. I don't want to be responsible for introducing anyone I know to someone who shows a high level of unprofessionalism on a regular basis. This, of course, should never happen, especially when we're talking about women of God. But it does. To me, we should never act out in an unethical, unkind, or dishonorable way. Not under any circumstances I can think of.

Not ever.

I know this because, when I was in my early thirties—thankfully well before the age of social media—I responded to someone, privately, by email, and it wasn't pretty. At the time, and for whatever reason, I totally disregarded what my first boss had taught me when I was a teenager, and I regretted it. Yes, back then, I had only been sixteen years old, and my part-time hostess position at Kentucky Fried Chicken only paid me minimum wage, but it was on my very first day of employment that I learned one of my most valuable lessons ever. It was when Joe, our store manager, told me "The customer is always right."

That was thirty-eight years ago, yet I can still hear Joe's words, and I will never forget them. To this day, I'm not sure why they resonated with me as much as they did, but even as an author, I have continued to honor that philosophy as much as I can, especially as it relates to my readers. I must admit, too, that when I'm paying for any service or product, and I discover that customer service isn't a company's priority, I become a little frustrated. Still, when I'm the one who is providing a product or service, I keep Joe's words at the forefront of my mind. I do this even when some readers post mean and spiteful comments about my books online or via social media.

But again, in my early thirties, I completely disregarded this philosophy, and when I received a brutal message from one of my readers, I reacted accordingly. I don't remember her name, but I do remember how I felt when I read her email. I remember how, for the most part, the woman had told me that one of my books was one of the worst stories she'd ever read. Then as if that weren't enough, she also talked about how awful the characters were and how the writing wasn't all that great, either. She'd sent me the harshest email I had ever received—and I could hardly finish reading the rest of her words fast enough before I began typing my response. So many thoughts paraded through my mind I didn't know what to begin with first. As a matter of fact, I was so upset that I even forwarded the woman's email to two other authors to see what they thought about it—realizing that I needed to hear someone else's opinion. Although, as much as they completely understood how I felt, they told me to ignore the woman and that I should *not* reply to her.

I so wish I could tell you that I listened to their great advice—because it absolutely *was* great advice—but I was also still very new to the publishing industry, and my relationship with God wasn't anywhere close to being where it is today. So the more I read the woman's email, the more hurt and wounded I became. I read it over and over, and each time I finished it, I added new words to my response. I even tried to explain why I had written the plot and the characters the way I had, hoping that she might reconsider the way she felt about my book. I tried to get her to like what I had written and to see things from my perspective—something that no author, singer, actress, artist, or any other creative should ever do.

But, sadly, I did do this. I tried to make my case, but as I wrote more and came closer to the end of my response, the pain I felt overrode every ounce of my professional nature, as well as the love and compassion I normally have for all others. I don't remember my exact words, but I do remember that I said something to the effect of "My guess is that the reason you have so much time to write such a long, vicious email is because you're probably lonely, miserable, and unhappy with your life." My reply to her was nothing nice, and if I'm being completely honest with myself, then I will also have to admit that it was cruel and immature. But because her words had hurt me so deeply, much more than they had angered me, I wanted to hurt her back.

Remember earlier in the book, when I talked about the friend who had screamed and cursed at me, yet I hadn't cursed back at her? Instead I had said hurtful things that I knew would cut her to her core? Well, I had done the same thing with this woman, which meant that this certainly hadn't turned out to be one of my finest hours. Worse, when she responded to my email, she didn't deny any of what I had described her as. She simply talked about how awful it was that, because she had given her honest opinion about my book, I had felt the need to attack her personally. This, however, suggested that maybe I had been right about some of what I had believed about her life, and this made me feel terrible. What I'd said to this woman was so wrong and disrespectful that I debated telling you about it now. But the reason I *am* sharing this is because my hope is that if you feel the need to defend yourself to anyone in a snarky, catty, malicious way, you'll think twice about it. I hope you'll be better than I was, because while this email exchange happened in the late nineties, and I didn't respond publicly the way so many women do on social media today, I am still very much ashamed of the way I reacted and behaved. This was all handled privately, yet I am still embarrassed about it, and I wish I could apologize to the woman personally. I was also especially ashamed because I wasn't raised that way, and I knew better. My grandmother had regularly told me to never do things "tit for tat," as she and my mom didn't believe in paying people back—no matter how terribly someone had treated them. But two decades ago, I still had a lot of learning and growing to do. I had, of course, always known that getting revenge was wrong, but when people make you feel bad, less than, not good enough, or unworthy, it can sometimes become very hard to ignore them. It can be difficult trying to move on without expressing our true feelings and easy to side with the enemy. We can even begin hoping that people get what *we* believe they have coming to them.

But I'm telling you, it is so not worth it.

I'm also asking you to think before you type any response to anyone, either on social media or via private messaging. I'm asking you to never involve yourself in online or in-person debates or disputes—or negative exchanges of any kind. Not with family, friends, or professional colleagues. I'm asking you to carry yourself in the wonderful way that God wants us to carry ourselves as women—women who love and honor Him.

Women whom He has given a purpose to.

This is what I had to remember myself, and after responding to the woman who contacted me, I became so much better. I realized that lashing out at her wasn't a good look for me, and that I wasn't practicing the Golden Rule. I also wasn't presenting my brand or platform in an honorable way. I wasn't showing myself in a way I could be proud of, but the good news is this: Many, many years ago, I stopped responding to those kinds of email messages, and whenever I do read negative comments about my work on bookstore or other literary websites, I keep it moving. I continue scrolling down the page or away from it altogether, because everyone has a right to like or not like something you've created. We all do. And unlike mean-spirited types of critiques, constructive criticism can be a good thing. It can help you grow in your gifts and abilities. So I make sure to remember all of this. I also remember what Joe told me. That the customer is always right—or in my case, my reading and speaking audiences are. Most of all, though, I remember who God wants me to be. I remember how He wants me to interact with others and how important it is for us to represent our brands, platforms, and reputations in the best way possible. All of which means offering great customer service and *being* of great service to others.

THREE THINGS YOU CAN DO

1. Be the same person behind closed doors and in public.

   Yep, this is a big one, and likely one of the most important pieces of advice I can give. I mean, we all know that, every now and then, there will be times when we might say or do something in private that we would never want anyone else to hear or see us do publicly. But these moments should be very limited. This is the reason that if you were to read every single comment I've ever posted on any of my social media pages, you won't find anything offensive, inappropriate, or distasteful. You also won't find any belligerent or insulting comments that I've posted on anyone else's page—and you won't find me treating people badly behind closed doors, either. Yes, as I mentioned earlier, there are times when I do become a little upset about blatant lack of customer service, but only because I believe we should all do the jobs we're being paid for—and I believe we should work hard at keeping our customers and clients happy, even if it means having to totally redo something. Not to mention, we should always arrive on time for any events we're invited to in a professional capacity, preferably a bit earlier than expected. Or if we're the ones hosting a meeting or an event, we should always start on time, because not doing so is very unfair to your attendees and it scars your reputation. Still, even when we find ourselves experiencing any of the above scenarios, we don't have to cause a scene, and we can handle these kinds of situations with dignity. We can continue being the same person privately and publicly, and for me, this also rings true as it relates to my Christian, moral, and family values. I will never be perfect, but even Will can tell you that I work hard at trying to do the right thing, regardless of who's watching and who isn't. I do this because, as I mentioned at the beginning of this book, even if no one else sees you doing the wrong thing, God sees you, and that's what matters most.

2. Remember that your client or customer is always right.

Please take this to heart. Please remember that your clients and customers are the reason you actually have a business or career. This holds true for ministry as well, because even when you are helping others, you need to treat them with the utmost respect. It is true that difficult people will sometimes complain about any- and everything, and nothing you do will satisfy them—even if you've done everything right—but you should still treat them in a courteous and amiable manner. You should still apologize and stay calm while speaking to them, and you should let them say whatever they feel they need to say. Then, you should evaluate their comments or complaints and decide whether you are doing everything correctly or if you might need to improve in a certain area. But, no matter what, please think before responding, and never allow your emotions to rule your thought process or make final decisions for you. This is where I failed all those years ago, and as you know, I regretted it. So, again, please think before responding, and handle any disagreements accordingly. Because I promise you, you'll be glad you did.

3. Don't let social media or tardiness become your greatest downfall.

I've talked quite a bit about social media, but because I'm seeing so many people post against business and professional protocol, I don't want to miss any opportunity to encourage women to do otherwise. We've already discussed inappropriate and offensive behavior, but what many women don't know is that posting photos of themselves every single day (or what they've eaten for breakfast, lunch, and dinner, or the luxury vehicle or expensive piece of jewelry they just purchased) isn't something that their clients or customers want to see on their business pages. If you are a fashion blogger or a clothing designer, then posting photos of yourself in various outfits is a must. If your business offers food or restaurant reviews, then posting numerous photos of your meals is fine. If you are a personal shopper or a clothing or jewelry retailer, then posting photos of certain luxury items makes total sense. But if you are frequently posting photos of yourself and everything else I've mentioned—or anything that has little to do with your business or ministry—daily, then you might want to tone things down a bit. Because even though many women believe that posting photos of themselves on a regular basis falls into the category of branding, you can sometimes "brand" yourself right out of business. Worse, many of your followers will begin wondering if your branding efforts are leaning more toward boasting, and you will soon notice them ignoring your page or unfollowing it. Don't get me wrong, sharing photos can be a good thing, and it can also be good for our platforms, but as women in ministry and business, we need to be discerning. We need to make sure we're not overdoing it.

A SCRIPTURE TO HELP YOU

"Show yourself in all respects to be a model of good works, and in your teaching show integrity, dignity..."

—TITUS 2:7 (ESV)

CHAPTER 18

Not Everyone Wishes You Well

I think the best way to begin this chapter is by telling you this: If people doubted and envied Jesus, they will certainly doubt and envy you. There's just no getting around it, and in Matthew 13:57 (NLT), even the Bible says, "And they were deeply offended and refused to believe in him. Then Jesus told them, 'A prophet is honored everywhere except in his own hometown and among his own family.'"

I love this scripture, because it, along with John 4:44, set me free. Jesus and His amazing words helped me understand why not everyone can be happy for us, and I've never looked back. When I was in my twenties, my mom told me, "Not everyone wishes you well," but I don't think I fully appreciated her wisdom on this subject until I was older. I didn't much focus on it at all until I began writing my first book—and telling a few people about it. It was then that I realized how right my mom was, because many of the reactions and responses I received were not what I had expected. Some people looked at me with a blank stare and no words to speak. Some forced themselves to say, "Oh, really?" and some simply said, "Oh, okay. Good for you," and then quickly moved on to a whole different conversation. They asked no questions at all and had no interest in learning more. They didn't want to know what I was writing about, why

I was even writing a book in the first place, or when I thought I would be finished. They mostly just stared at me, seemingly thinking what a crazy, farfetched idea it was. I could tell that some at least thought it was a nice dream to have, but also that I would never see it come to pass. Then, there were those who looked at me as though I were some naïve child, fantasizing about something that could never happen in a trillion years.

So, this, my friend, is the reason I stopped telling anyone anything about the book I was working on—that is, with the exception of Will, my mom, my brothers, a couple of other family members, and two of my closest friends, all of whom were excited and supportive during the entire process. But with everyone else, I had to keep my goals and dreams to myself, because if I hadn't, I knew I would give up. I knew that if I continued to see some of the discouraging, dissuading looks and hearing some of the doubtful, disbelieving comments, I would shut everything down. I knew I would lose all confidence, not only in the plan that God had for me, but also in myself and in what I was writing about.

Staying quiet about my work and only sharing it with the people I mentioned above is what gave me the courage to continue. Surrounding myself only with people who had no reason to envy me or want the worst for me—people who cheered me on—is what kept me going. All the way until I finished. But then, as you know, once I began submitting to literary agents and then ultimately to publishing houses, I was rejected by everyone. Not a single agent or editor was interested in taking me on, and of course, I couldn't help thinking back to some of the initial people I had told that I was writing a book. I couldn't stop myself from wondering if maybe they'd been right to think how ridiculous my attempt had been, and that maybe failure was all I could hope for.

This is the reason I want *you*, my dear sister, to do things differently. This is the reason I want you to discover your purpose, and when you begin executing my 4-P Process, I want you to pray for God's protection. I want you to ask Him to reveal to you whom you can trust. Ask Him to show you which of your family and friends will support you and help you reach your goals. What I want is for you to figure out who those people are and share your progress only with them. That way, when you experience your own moments of doubt, you'll have each of them to turn to. You'll have a small tribe—because believe me, in the beginning, it will be microscopically small—but that tiny tribe will include the wonderfully loyal, dedicated people who want the best for you. You'll have an amazing circle of allies who will root you on and tell you that giving up is not an option.

You'll be blessed to have the kind of people that God gave me—those who encouraged me to start my own business so that I could publish the book myself. But guess what? Even after I moved forward with doing so and once the initial book covers arrived, I made the mistake of showing them to a couple of folks who still hadn't wished me well the way I had hoped. One person said to me, "Wow, this is a real book," and the other said, "Oh, I was thinking that maybe you were just writing some sort of pamphlet. You know, something for family." I remember not knowing how to feel about either comment, because not once had I said I wasn't writing a real book or that I was writing a pamphlet for relatives.

Nonetheless, this stopped me from talking about it any further, except to people who were fully on board with helping me and those who were—yes, here's that word again—*encouraging* me. I stayed focused, planned my opening reception, and proceeded with getting my book on the shelves of bookstores. But then, as you also know, after the reception, Will suggested that I resign from my job, and I did. I stepped out on faith, more than I ever had before, but can you believe there were still people who just couldn't understand why I had quit? Why I had given up full-time employment to work from home? One person even asked Will, "How does a person work from *home*?" and then laughed a little about it. I believe this person had decided that, even though my book release reception had gone well, I would eventually fail on a national level. Oh, and I won't even go into my full story about the person who called me on the phone directly just to tell me that someone didn't think the author photo I had used on my book was a good one. She'd then gone on to tell me that she'd heard other comments, too, but thankfully, she didn't elaborate on them. I was stunned and hurt, and from then on, I never called her again. She stopped calling me, too, and that was good, because the last thing I needed was having to converse with someone who was purposely trying to condemn what I was trying to accomplish.

And if that weren't enough, a few men in town came at Will out of nowhere. These were men he'd known for a very long time, which is the reason that, even as I'm writing this, it's still hard for me to fathom, because, let's be honest, some men might be haters, but they don't tend to express their hate or envy out loud. At least not as quickly as some women might do. Nonetheless, a few months after I self-published my book, there was a group of men who asked Will the following: "Man, with the way your wife's writing career is going, do you really think she's going to stay with you? Can you imagine all the other men she'll have a chance to meet in other cities?"

"What? You can't be serious." Those were my responses to Will, because every bit of what he was telling me was astonishing. These grown men were taunting him and laughing about their ludicrous predictions, and those jokes and taunts didn't make Will feel all that great—until I reminded him that by the time I had finally sat down to write the first word of my book, I had already been in love with him and married to him for five whole years. Not to mention, from the start, my writing and publishing career has always been a team effort, and Will has given me more business and storyline advice than most people realize. But more important, no career, job, or any amount of money will ever take priority over him.

I knew that then. I know it now. I always will.

Still, this was yet one more example of people not wishing us well, and I don't think some people can help it. Some people are simply being who they are. So, if you find that family, friends, or acquaintances don't support your goals and dreams, just know that their ill feelings are likely not about you. Know that it is mostly about them, and that, sadly, your success may be reminding *them* of what *they're* not doing. It may also be confirming that, unlike you, they're afraid to step out on radical faith. They're afraid to trust and believe God. They're afraid to be different. They're terrified of doing something unconventional, even if God has given them everything they need to be victorious. But no matter what their reason is, their lack of faith isn't your fault. What they say about you is not your business, and you should never feel the need to apologize about anything that God has called you to do. Because if you do allow naysayers to get inside your head, they will talk you out of everything you have confidence in. They will stifle your progress, and before long, you'll find yourself trusting and believing *them* more than you trust and believe God. So instead of allowing any of that to happen, I am encouraging you to do this: "Believe in God, believe in yourself, believe in whatever it is you are trying to accomplish ... believe in that order."

This is my own personal quote, and it is also the philosophy I live by daily—in that order. I believe in God because He reigns above all else, and because I know, beyond a shadow of a doubt, that I can't do *anything* without Him. I believe in myself, because if I don't, others won't believe in me, either— and because with the exception of God, no one can be a better advocate for me than I can be for myself. Then, finally, I believe in whatever I am trying to accomplish, because if I believe otherwise, my chances of success are null and void from the start.

So, please: Believe, believe, believe—even if you're the only one who does.

THREE THINGS YOU CAN DO

1. Surround yourself with people you can trust.

Please make this a priority. You should also surround yourself with people who will support you until the end of time. Surround yourself with people who have shown, year after year, that they have your back through good times and bad—people who will be there for you, day or night, when you need them, even if only to listen. Many times, this will include family members or people you have known since elementary school or since your high school or college days, but you can also meet trustworthy friends and colleagues later in life. If you do, please pray for discernment, and pay attention to their words and actions. Notice how they treat other friends, colleagues, and their family, and if they ever show themselves to be untrustworthy—in any way—don't think it's some sort of fluke. Don't tell yourself it's a one-time thing. Because as Maya Angelou so profoundly stated, "When people show you who they are, believe them." Believe them, and move on before you regret it.

2. Don't worry about who's not supporting you.

Very few days go by when I don't see someone posting about people who don't support others. This is not something I can relate to, as it has never occurred to me to become angry at anyone who has never purchased one of my books, attended any of my events, or clicked "like" on one of my social media posts (posts they may not have actually seen anyway). More important, though, not everything is for everybody. So, please don't become angry with folks simply because they told you no about something or because they haven't supported your ministries, businesses, or events the way you want them to. Sometimes people just aren't able to do so. Sometimes people have other engagements, responsibilities, or financial obligations that will prevent them from being there for you in a way you expect. I know, for me, I am sometimes unable to support people for many different reasons, even when I wish my schedule would allow me to. I honestly believe that instead of focusing on who hasn't supported us, we should gear that time and energy toward the people who *are* supporting us, and we should also concentrate on reaching people outside of our local and regional areas. Because as long as we are fulfilling our purpose and serving others, it doesn't matter how far away they reside from us. And please don't forget—not even Jesus received the kind of support that He expected from his own town of Galilee, yet He didn't let that stop Him. Likely because sometimes when people know you personally or they see you all the time, they're not impressed. Sometimes they can only see you as the little girl they've known for decades or as the young woman they've chatted with in Target or Walmart for years. Sometimes they can't picture you doing anything out of the ordinary. But we can't worry about that. We can't focus on the negative opinions of others. Yes, our belief in what we're doing may cause some folks to laugh, ridicule, or shake their heads at us like we're crazy, but as long as we're doing what God has called us to do, we're good.

3. Never give up.

As I'm sure you'll remember, I was very close to giving up on my first book. But what if I had? What if I'd filed my manuscript in a drawer or thrown it away altogether and gone back to corporate America? What if my mom hadn't told me that I *shouldn't* give up? What if Will hadn't encouraged me to self-publish or convinced me to leave my full-time job? What if I had simply walked away from what I knew in my heart I was destined to do? Well, let me tell you—I wouldn't have published my debut novel, *Behind Closed Doors*... I wouldn't have sold ten thousand copies within the first six months... I wouldn't have found a literary agent... She wouldn't have sold my second book to a New York publishing house ... I wouldn't have written twenty-seven books in a twenty-two-year time span ... I wouldn't have made the *New York Times* bestseller list as many times as I did ... And I certainly wouldn't have written this book, my first nonfiction title. I also wouldn't have had the opportunity to connect with readers everywhere or experience the love and kindness they have shown me for years. So please don't give up. On God, yourself, or your purpose. Keep going—until you accomplish everything you've set out to do.

A SCRIPTURE TO HELP YOU

"For Jesus Himself testified that a prophet has no honor in his own country."

—JOHN 4:44 (NKJV)

CHAPTER 19

Be Hugely Successful Without Jeopardizing Your Faith

One of the best things I have ever done was void a check from my literary agency that included a $100,000 overpayment. It had only been a few months since Elaine, my longtime agent and founder of the agency, had passed away. But when I received the bank draft, opened it, and saw that the check had been written for far more than I was supposed to receive, I didn't wait for anyone else to discover it. Instead, I immediately called the office, notified them, and waited for them to send me the correct amount. That was in January 2011, but not long ago, I pulled the statement from a file, which has the voided check attached to it, and smiled. It warmed my heart, and it made me think about my mom and grandmother—the women who raised me to do the right thing, no matter what. Yes, it would have been nice to add every dime of that massive overpayment to Will's and my savings account, but this was never a consideration, because I knew it didn't belong to me.

I voided the check and never thought twice about it, and since that time, God has blessed Will and me in more ways than I can explain—all of which has allowed us to be a blessing to others.

Then, there is the fact that I have passed on three film/TV offers for my Reverend Curtis Black series. Not many people know about this, because I don't speak of it very often, but over the last six years, I was approached by a division of a major motion picture company for a movie option, by one of the original big-three TV networks for a television series, and by an independent production company for a TV series option. Actually, for the independent offer, I did agree to a one-year option, but when it expired, I decided to pass on renewing it. And the reason I passed on the first two altogether, after reviewing the printed agreements, was because no one would contractually guarantee that none of the dialogue or scenes would cross certain lines— the kind of lines that I would never cross, as they relate to my Christian, moral, and family values. And no, I didn't want any form of production control, but I did want to have an opportunity to read every script and be able to request a revision for anything that would offend me or my reading audience. There is no doubt that Reverend Curtis Black and many of the other characters in the book series have done a lot—and that's putting it nicely—but they have never done any more than what I have allowed them to do. Because for me, some sinful depictions and scenarios are off limits, and no amount of money is worth jeopardizing the values I just mentioned. What's important to me is that I present my work with as much integrity as possible, so that I can sleep peacefully at bedtime.

But don't get me wrong, I was very excited and grateful to receive each of the three offers, and what I know for sure is that if God wants my work to appear on the big or small screen, it will. He will allow it to happen in His timing and in the manner that He wants it to be portrayed. Or if having a movie or TV deal is not what He wants for me, I'm good with that, too.

My Christian, moral, and family values are also the reason I could no longer include profanity in my novels. I spoke briefly about this in Chapter 2, but what I didn't share was how this wonderful change came to be. It was the year that I sat down to begin writing my tenth book, sometime in 2006, which was also the fifth book in my Reverend Curtis Black series. As always, I wrote a two-to-three-page synopsis and then created a pretty detailed outline. But then, when it was time for me to begin writing the actual chapters, I couldn't seem to get going. For the first time in my career, I seemed to have writer's block, something I had never much experienced before. I would pray, then sit in front of my computer and just stare at it. I would attempt to write the first sentence and then delete it. I would browse the Internet or Myspace, as this was two years before I finally joined Facebook and one year before joining Twitter—but I would browse, read a few articles, check email, and then return to my manuscript. Still, nothing came to me that seemed like a good way to begin my story, and I became worried. I prayed, but God wasn't giving me what I needed to write any of the chapters I had outlined. And it was then that I began questioning my purpose and whether God wanted me to continue writing at all. I wondered if nine storylines were all I had in me, and if maybe it was time to move on to something else. I even shared my thoughts with Will and Kelli, because I honestly thought my novel-writing days had ended.

But then, I prayed about it once more, and God spoke to my mind, heart, and spirit. This was another one of the few times that I have heard His words just as clearly as when I am thinking my own thoughts. It was very similar to the swift way He answered my question about whether I should submit the book you're reading now to my publisher or self-publish it. But this time, when I asked Him to give me the words He wanted me to write, he responded to my question *with* a question. "Why are you including words that you don't use yourself?" I heard those words, thought about them, and I felt liberated. This was such a huge relief and revelation for me, that I also asked *myself* a question: *Why am I writing the kind of intimate scenes in my books that I don't like reading?*

So, from that day on, I decided that I wouldn't include profanity or any graphic sex scenes, no matter how much I had believed that my scenes were "tasteful." That's how I used to refer to them, because they weren't as graphic as what I knew was being written in some other books. But, as we all know, it is very easy to justify doing something we believe we should do, even if it's wrong. Especially when we feel the need to do it for money. I say this because the only reason I wrote certain words and scenes that didn't align with my Christian values was because I didn't think I could sell very many books without them. I was worried that my readers would think my stories were boring and not worth reading. But as I've mentioned before, God always knows what He's doing.

And He blesses us for being obedient.

Because, as it turned out, the hardcover edition of *Sin No More* was released with my highest-ever first printing. Even better, after God delivered me from writing inappropriate words and scenes, my words flowed daily while writing *Sin No More* and for each of my books thereafter. I also believe that this will continue to be one of my most memorable John 15 moments, particularly John 15:1–4 (NIV), which states, "I am the true vine, and my Father is the gardener. He cuts off every branch in me that bears no fruit, while every branch that does bear fruit he prunes so that it will be even more fruitful. You are already clean because of the word I have spoken to you. Remain in me, as I also remain in you. No branch can bear fruit by itself; it must remain in the vine. Neither can you bear fruit unless you remain in me."

God took me through an amazing pruning process. He gave me what I needed when I needed it, and because I have grown spiritually and I work hard to do what He wants me to do—and I choose not to lie, cheat, steal, or deceive others to get ahead—I believe God has protected me during all the years of my professional life. In business, I have never tried to manipulate or take advantage of anyone, because it's just not necessary, and it's not who I am. More important, it's wrong. So please know that *you* don't ever have to lie, cheat, steal, deceive, manipulate, or take advantage of anyone, either. You don't have to do any of that to accomplish your goals or carry out the purpose that God has given you.

And you can still be hugely successful without jeopardizing your faith.

You can still live your very best life.

As women of God, we can do all of this and more, as long as we trust and honor Him completely.

THREE THINGS YOU CAN DO

1. Be honest, and always do the right thing.

This reminds me of the time back in the early nineties when I'd left work and driven to the Burger King restaurant near our apartment complex. I'm sure you remember how much I once loved eating fast food burgers. Anyway, I rolled toward the drive-thru speaker, placed my order for a burger and fries, and continued toward the window. Once I was there, a young woman told me how much I owed, I paid her, and she passed me my change and receipt. After that, I waited a few minutes, and soon, she passed me my bag of food, along with a medium-size soda. I slowly started to drive away, but then it dawned on me that I hadn't ordered a soda. I also didn't remember seeing a charge for one on my receipt. But as I sat there in those brief seconds, debating whether I should shift my car in reverse and back up to the window, I continued driving forward and out of the parking lot. I can't remember why I hadn't ordered a soda, but if I were to guess, I'd say that I likely had some sort of soda at home that the restaurant didn't offer. Nonetheless, I drove away, and when I arrived in my own parking lot, I gathered my belongings and my food and drink from the car and went inside our apartment building. My hands were somewhat full, but I still stopped in the entryway, opened our designated mailbox with my key, pulled out our mail, and went upstairs to our second-floor apartment. But then it happened. I turned the key inside our door, and my "free" drink crashed to the floor, splattering everywhere. Soda and ice flooded the carpeted hallway, and some of it even splashed on me. But as soon as all of this occurred, the first thing that entered my mind was the fact that I hadn't paid for that soda. I also hadn't done the right thing, which was to let the young woman at the window know about it—offering her a chance to either charge me accordingly or tell me the soda was on the house, which is what some hostesses or waitresses will say if your bill has already been paid. But from that day on, I have never walked away with anything I didn't see on my paid receipts. I take this very seriously, and not more than two years ago, when my twin niece and nephew and I were in Bath & Body Works, walking toward the exit, I scanned my receipt. And when I noticed that the salesclerk hadn't charged me for the two liquid soap holders I had purchased, the three of us turned around and went back to the counter so that I could inform the sales clerk about it. I would have done this whether my teenage niece and nephew were with me or not, but that day, I was glad it happened, so that hopefully they, too, will remember to *always* be honest and do the right thing—no matter how big or small the circumstance may seem.

2. Never take advantage of others.

Not on any day of the week should we cheat, steal, or try to take advantage of anyone. And many people who know me personally have likely heard me say out loud, "I'm not doing that." This is usually when someone has suggested an easier way for me to accomplish something, and it involves getting over in one way or another. Or someone has subtly suggested that I cut out a person who has initiated a business deal with me and go around them altogether. I have had this happen a couple of times, and not only was I mortified, but I never looked at those people the same again. Being honest and showing compassion for everyone is always the right thing to do, and just as I've said before—we can still be hugely successful without jeopardizing our faith.

3. Remember that not all money is good money.

I've shared with you the reasons that I've not signed with a
motion picture studio or a major television network for my
Reverend Curtis Black series, and as you know, the main
reason is that I don't want to sacrifice any of my values for
money. I don't want to sell my soul or do anything that goes
against everything I believe in, just for the sake of notoriety
or a larger bank account. Yes, of course, I want to be a successful woman of God, because I don't see anything wrong
with that. But I also want to continue earning my living in
an honest way. I want to do things in a manner that I can be
proud of. I want to be an example to women of all ages, letting them know that honesty really is the best policy. I know
that statement is cliché, but it says everything because when
we are honest, we show ourselves to be honorable. When we
show compassion, we show love to others. When we treat
others the way we want to be treated, we show ourselves to
be true women of God. If we do all of this, we will earn the
right kind of money in the right kind of way, and we won't
have to do anything that isn't good for us. We can do the
right thing and still be fine.

A SCRIPTURE TO HELP YOU

"There is joy for those who deal justly with others and always
do what is right."

—PSALM 106:3 (NLT)

CONCLUSION

The Total You

Writing this book has been a wonderful journey, and I hope it has been a blessing to you in more ways than one. My prayer is that each chapter has inspired and motivated you to become the very best that you can be in all areas of your life. What I hope, too, is that you will think about which of those areas you believe you should focus on first and start there. If you need to become better spiritually, then I am encouraging you to reread Chapters 1 through 6. If you believe your spiritual life is in order but you are struggling personally, I would recommend rereading Chapters 7 through 13. Or if you find that you are doing well spiritually and personally, but your professional life isn't where it needs to be, then please reread Chapters 14 through 19.

In the Introduction, I talked about how important it was for us to keep our faith at the center of everything. Why? Because it is our faith in God that will help us mentally, emotionally, and physically. With God, we can do the impossible—for such a time as this—and step fully into our purpose. We can experience total excellence, the kind that only He can provide. We can become our absolute best, spiritually, personally, and professionally—so that we can use every gift, talent, skill, and ability that God has given each of us ... so that we can live out our dreams at *any* age—any age at all—and help others do the same ... so that we can take better care of ourselves and be there for our family and friends ... so that we can move forward, enjoying life and serving others in a way that will glorify God at the highest levels.

So that we can become the amazing women God created us to be!

Acknowledgments

To my Heavenly Father. Lord, I thank You for giving me the desire, motivation, and determination to write and publish my twenty-eighth book —and for allowing my passion for helping women to become the center of my purpose. Your unconditional love, mercy, and grace continue to bless all areas of my life, and I am eternally grateful to You for everything. I thank You for just being You.

Then, to my dearest Roby. Of course, not everyone knows that Roby has always been my daily nickname for you, so for that reason, I have referred to you only as Will in the book. But thank you for being the love of my life, as well as the most supportive and protective husband ever. For twenty-nine years, you have loved me and been there for me in every way imaginable, and I thank God for you a thousand times over. You have been the husband of a lifetime—marrying you was certainly the best decision I ever made—and I love you with every part of my being.

To the best mom ever, Arletha Tennin Stapleton, and the best grandparents ever, Clifton Tennin, Sr. and Mary Tennin. After all these years, I still miss all three of you in such an enormous way, but I am so incredibly grateful to God for allowing you to be here with me for as long as He did. I certainly wish it could have been longer—much, much longer—but I so appreciate everything you taught me and did for me, as well as, how you loved me in such an absolute and very special way. What I find peace in, too, is knowing that you are home with God, and that I will see you again. I love you, Mom, Grandma, and Grandad, forever.

To my dear brother and sister-in-law, Willie Jr. and April Stapleton, and my dear brother, Michael Stapleton. To my bonus son, daughter-in-law, and grandsons: Trenod Vines-Roby, LaTasha Vines, Alex Lamont Knight, and Trenod Vines, Jr. To my brothers-in-law and sisters-in-law: Gloria Roby, Ronald Roby, Terry and Karen Roby, Robert and Tammy Roby. To my aunts and uncles: Ben Tennin, Fannie Haley, Ada Tennin, Mary Lou Beasley (you are truly missed), Charlie Beasley, Vernell Tennin, Ollie Tennin, Marie Tennin, Shirley Jean Gary, Ed Gary, Ruby Gary, Lehman Gary, Thressia Gary, Rosie Norman, and Isaac Gary. To all my cousins and other family members (every single one of you!): Tennins, Ballards, Lawsons, Stapletons, Beasleys, Haleys, Greens, Robys, Garys, Shannons, and Normans—I love all of you so very much, and thank you for everything.

To my dear first cousin and sister, Patricia Haley-Glass; my two dear best friends and sisters, Kelli Tunson Bullard and Lori Whitaker Thurman; my dear cousin and sister, Janell Green; my dear fellow authors and sisters, Trisha R. Thomas, Trice Hickman-Hayes, Marissa Monteilh, and Cheryl Polote-Williamson; my long-time, dear friends and sisters, Venita Sockwell Owens, Gwyn Gulley, Pamela Hanserd, Danetta Taylor, Karen Young Coleman, Eleanor Brown Prunty, Karen R. Thomas, Connie Dettman, Pamela Charles Gibson, Venae Fowler Jackson, Janet Salter, Shandra Hill Smith, Claudia

Parker, and Linda Duggins; and my dear book club members and sisters of twenty years: Regina Taylor, Cathrine Watkins, Valerie Hanserd, Cookie Givens, Mattie Holden, and Emily Sanders—thank you, ladies, for always being there for me. I love you all so very much.

To Pastor K. Edward Copeland, First Lady Starla Copeland, and our entire New Zion Missionary Baptist Church family; to my wonderful spiritual mom and family: Dr. Betty Price, Apostle Frederick K.C. Price, Angela Evans, Cheryl Price, Stephanie Buchanan, Pastor Fred Price, Jr., Angel Price, and the entire Crenshaw Christian Center family—thank you all for everything, and I love you dearly.

To my amazing first readers, the women who took precious time from their busy schedules to read this book and offer such encouraging and helpful feedback: Dr. Betty Price, Lori Whitaker Thurman, Janell Green, Connie Dettman, LaTasha Vines, Danetta Taylor, Trisha R. Thomas, and Kelli Tunson Bullard—you ladies have no idea how much I appreciate your being there for me when I really needed your input and overall opinion. Thank you for everything.

To my awesome editing and production team: Karen R. Thomas (content editor), Laura Cherkas (copyeditor), Chandra Sparks Splond (proofreader), Sonya Martin (cover photographer), Laura Duffy (graphic designer), and Karen Minster (book designer). From the start, I knew I wanted this particular book—that I was writing *for* women—to be produced by women. So, thank you for your wonderful professionalism, expertise, and kindness throughout this entire process, as I couldn't have done any of this without you.

To my marketing and website team: Pamela Walker-Williams and Sharvette Mitchell. Thanks a million for all you do for me. I so appreciate you ladies.

With all my love and many blessings to everyone,

Kimberla

About the Author

Kimberla Lawson Roby is a *New York Times* Bestselling Author & Speaker who has published 28 books, including *Casting the First Stone, Better Late Than Never, A Christmas Prayer, It's a Thin Line*, and her debut title, *Behind Closed Doors*, which she originally self-published through her own company. Kimberla's books have frequented numerous bestseller lists, such as *The New York Times, USA Today, The Washington Post, Publishers Weekly, Essence, Black Christian News*, Amazon, Barnes & Noble, and many others. She is the recipient of the 2013 NAACP Image Award for Outstanding Literary Work–Fiction and the 2017 SOAR Radio Trailblazer of Honor award.

Over the years, Kimberla has spoken to thousands of women at churches, conferences, luncheons, libraries, colleges, and universities where she candidly shares her personal journey— hoping to help women become all that God created them to be.

Kimberla resides in Illinois with her husband, Will.

Website: kimroby.com
Facebook.com/kimberlalawsonroby
Instagram.com/kimberlalawsonroby
Twitter.com/KimberlaLRoby

Made in the USA
Monee, IL
30 August 2021